PSYCHOLOGY PERSPECTIVES

FOR THE CHICANO AND LATINO FAMILY

FIRST EDITION

By Yvette Flores
University of California - Davis

cognella®
academic publishing

Bassim Hamadeh, CEO and Publisher
Michael Simpson, Vice President of Acquisitions
Jamie Giganti, Managing Editor
Miguel Macias, Graphic Designer
Kristina Stolte, Acquisitions Editor
Michelle Piehl, Project Editor
Alexa Lucido, Licensing Coordinator
Mandy Licata, Interior Designer

First published in the United States of America in 2015 by Cognella, Inc.

Printed in the United States of America

ISBN: 978-1-63189-108-3 (pbk) / 978-1-63189-109-0 (br)

cognella
academic publishing
www.cognella.com 800-200-3908

CONTENTS

ACKNOWLEDGMENTS

This book could not have been written without the support of my family. With deep gratitude to my original *familia*: my parents, may they rest in peace; my biological children, Xochitl Maria Henninger (nee Ortiz) and Alejandro Esteban Ortiz; my stepchildren, Britt Ortiz and Brigitte De Mille Ortiz; my son-in-law, Tyron Henninger; my granddaughters, Jessica and Melina Virgen Ortiz, Lei-Lahni Xitlali, and Naturelly Idolly Henninger; and my grandsons, Jaali and Tyron Rommello Henninger. I also recognize the invaluable assistance of my extended family and the seven generations who came before me. We are connected by blood and spirit.

This book would not have been possible without the support and encouragement of my circle of friends who nurture and support me: Drs. Hector Rivera-Lopez, Beatriz Pesquera, Lesleigh Franklin, Ellen Lanzone, Regina Armas, and Rosa Granadillo-Schwentker; Vilma Wilcoxen, MA, MFT; and Marisol Reyna, MA. All of these colleagues are a source of continued inspiration.

I also dedicate this book to the many generations of students I have had the privilege to teach, especially Monica Siañez, MPH, DrPH; Rosa Manzo, PhD: and Rosa Gomez-Camacho, PhD: to my research assistant and dedicated alum, Briza Ramirez; to my professional *familia* in Chicana and Chicano Studies at U.C. Davis, Carlos Jackson, MFA; Maceo Montoya, MFA; Natalia Deeb Sossa, PhD; Angie Chabram, PhD; Sergio de la Mora, PhD.; Susie Zepeda, PhD. and Clarissa Rojas, PhD., and Vice Chancellor of Student Affairs, Adela de la Torre, PhD.

And, finally, to our Chicana/o Studies staff, Alyssa West and Alma Martinez, your commitment to students and building *familia* is a source of inspiration.

INTRODUCTION

LATINO FAMILIES IN THE TWENTY-FIRST CENTURY: CHALLENGES AND OPPORTUNITIES

Chicano/Latino Families in Context

In the first decade of the twenty-first century, 50.5 million Latinos[1] lived in the United States, constituting the largest ethnic minority group in the country and accounting for more than 50 percent of the population growth since the 2000 Census (US Census 2010; Pew Research Center 2010). By 2012, Latinos had increased to 53 million (News 2013). Latinos in the United States comprise a racial tapestry reflecting the population demographics of the 21 countries that comprise the Americas. The largest subgroup of US Latinos are of Mexican origin (65 percent). Only Mexico had a larger "Hispanic" population than the United States in 2010 with 112 million (US Census International Data). Another 9.4 percent of US Latino residents were of Puerto Rican background, 3.8 percent Salvadoran, 3.6 percent Cuban, 3.0 percent Dominican, and 2.3 percent Guatemalan. The remainder was of some other Central American, South American, or other Hispanic/Latino origin (US Census 2011).

According to the Pew Research Center, there were 17.1 million Latinos ages 17 or younger living in the US in 2012, constituting 23.1 percent of children in that age group; this represented a 39 percent increase in the number of Latino children since 2000. The adult population (Latinos over the age of 18) was 33.3 million in 2010; this represents a 45 percent increase from 2000. While immigration to the United States from Latin America contributed to the population increase, the majority of Latinos were born in the US. In 2010, only 36.2 percent of Latinos were foreign born.

By 2012, there were 11.6 million Latino households in the United States. Of these, 63.2 percent were heterosexual married couples and 60.4 percent had children younger than 18 years of age. Furthermore, 65.7 percent of Latino children were living with two parents in 2012; 45.3 percent of Latino children lived in households where both parents worked outside the home (US Census Bureau, 2012). The same report noted that 37.6 million Latino residents older than five years of age spoke Spanish at home; more than half of those residents reported also speaking English very well. Thus, Latino families often comprise a significant number of bilingual households in the United States[2].

While divorce rates have escalated in the past few decades among European Americans, the majority of Latinos marry or form long-term domestic partnerships, remain married, and have children. However, their family formations are diverse and face a myriad of challenges and disparities related to the degree of structural integration to US society they have attained (Rumbaut 1994; Portes 1993). The most salient of the disparities is related to their economic position. In 2001, the median family income for Latinos was $38,264, whereas the mean household income for the country was $62,273 (US Census Bureau 2011). Overall, the mean household income declined for all United States citizens between 2011–2012. Furthermore, there were differences in family income throughout the country with the western United States experiencing the greatest decline. For example, Mexican origin families in congressional district 20 (CD 20), which includes the agricultural-rich central valley of California, is considered the poorest in the country. Based on the Human Development Index (De La Torre 2013), the district had a median family income of $25,441. While the nation's official poverty rate in 2011 was 15.0 percent with 46.2 million people living in poverty, the poverty rate among Latinos was 25.3%. This figure represented a slight decline in poverty rates since the previous year.

Family income is related to the types of jobs performed and level of education attained. Among Latinos, there is significant variability in educational attainment, depending on nativity and generational status. In 2012, 34% of US Latinos ages 25–29 held a high school diploma. Only 12% of that same population held a baccalaureate degree, 2% held a master's degree, and only 0.18% held a doctoral degree. In comparison, 30% of all Whites ages 25–29 held a high school diploma, 20% held a baccalaureate degree, 8.1% held a master's degree, and 1.6% held a doctoral degree (US Census 2012). Of the various Latino population groups, Chicanos had the lowest educational attainment and one of the highest high school discontinuation rates (Manzo, 2014). Such lack of educational advancement may account for the fact that in 2011 only 19.2 percent of Latinos 16 and older worked in management, business, science, and the arts. The majority of Latinos, 67.4 percent, worked in civilian jobs (including blue collar and service categories). Large numbers of Latinos, particularly immigrants from rural areas of Mexico, worked in agriculture. Latinos also have high rates of participation in the military; in 2011, 1.8 million Latinos were either active military personnel or veterans of the US armed forces.

Job categories also influence overall health as many Latinos are underinsured or have no access to health insurance. According to the US Census (2010), 30.1 percent of Latinos lacked health insurance. However, if the data are disaggregated by nativity and job category, then Mexican immigrants and agricultural workers face significantly greater health disparities based on lack of access to health care (De la Torre 2010; Flores 2014).

Access to good schooling and well-paid jobs, which may provide individual and family health insurance, also is impacted by citizenship status. While the majority of Latinos are citizens or residents, large numbers also reside in the United States without status. It is estimated that unauthorized immigrants made up 28% of all US immigrants in 2012, down from 30% in 2007 (Pew Research Center 2013). The same report notes that most unauthorized migration is of Mexicans.

Clearly, Mexican origin and other Latinos will continue to constitute a significant proportion of residents of the United States. Therefore, it is crucial to understand their psychosocial characteristics and the ways in which families support and prepare the ever-growing population of Latino children in US schools.

This book provides an overview of the major issues affecting Latino families today and offers a review of theoretical models that promote an understanding of these issues. In particular, I engage theories that explain how migration and the multigenerational legacies of previous migrations, including the conquest of the Americas, nuance family patterns and contribute to family injustice when it exists. In addition, the book highlights how nativity, race, ethnicity, sexuality, religion, spirituality, and cultural values influence gender roles, parenting styles, and the negotiation of power in family relations within and across generations of Chicana/os and Latina/os.

The book is grounded in family psychology. According to the American Psychological Association, Division 45,

> *Family Psychology is a specialty in professional psychology that is focused on the emotions, thoughts, and behavior of individuals, couples, and families in relationships and in the broader environment in which they function.*

Family Psychology as a Theoretical Foundation

Family psychology is founded on principles of systems theory (Gurman 1991) whereby the family as a system is considered the most central focus of study and intervention. Family psychology emerged as an important sub-discipline in the 1960s when a group of psychologists and psychiatrists working with socioeconomically and ethnically diverse populations in the United States began to address the limitations of individual psychology and related psychotherapy approaches in the treatment of people with schizophrenia and other mental health problems. Working in Philadelphia with African American and Puerto Rican families in the late 1950s and early 1960s, Salvador Minuchin, an Argentinean psychoanalytically trained psychiatrist, began to study non-White families and argued that families must be studied, understood, and treated with consideration of their social class, race, and ethnicity[3]. Twenty years later, McGoldrick, Giordano, and Pearce (Guilford Press 1982) published the classic text, *Ethnicity and Family Therapy*, now in its third edition with Nydia Garcia-Preto as co-author (McGoldrick 2005). This book brought the intersection of race, class, and ethnicity to the forefront of family psychology. Furthermore, by addressing the role of culture and ethnicity in the development and functioning of European American families as well as families of color, the authors contested the supposition held by many mental health professionals that culture and ethnicity were relevant factors only for non-dominant culture individuals, which often resulted in blaming the culture and/or ethnicity for the dysfunction in families that were poor and socially marginalized. At the same time, feminist psychologists were foregrounding the importance of gender in the functioning of families, particularly in terms of understanding culturally rooted power dynamics (Goodrich 1988).

Over the past quarter century, family psychology has become a well-respected discipline with professional organizations [4], degree granting institutions, and thousands of publications worldwide. Family psychology is particularly useful to understand the emotional and psychological well-being of Latinos, given the cultural importance of *familia* (family). The privileging of the family unit as the most important social organization for Latinos has its roots in both indigenous and Spanish cultural legacies (Flores 2013). The models presented in this book have generated best practices for the treatment of Latino families with problems rooted in their social location and migration legacies, as well as intergenerational trauma related to historical experiences with conquest and domination and the sequelae of more recent social, political, and intrafamily violence both in the US and abroad.

As McGoldrick has noted, to understand individual human beings we must comprehend them in the context of their family, which is situated within a community that is part of the larger society. In addition, it is also critical to examine the history of individuals and determine how past experiences may have impacted their current family formation and individual psychology, as well as the influence of history and intergenerational legacies on the development of contemporary individual and family problems. For Latinos, as

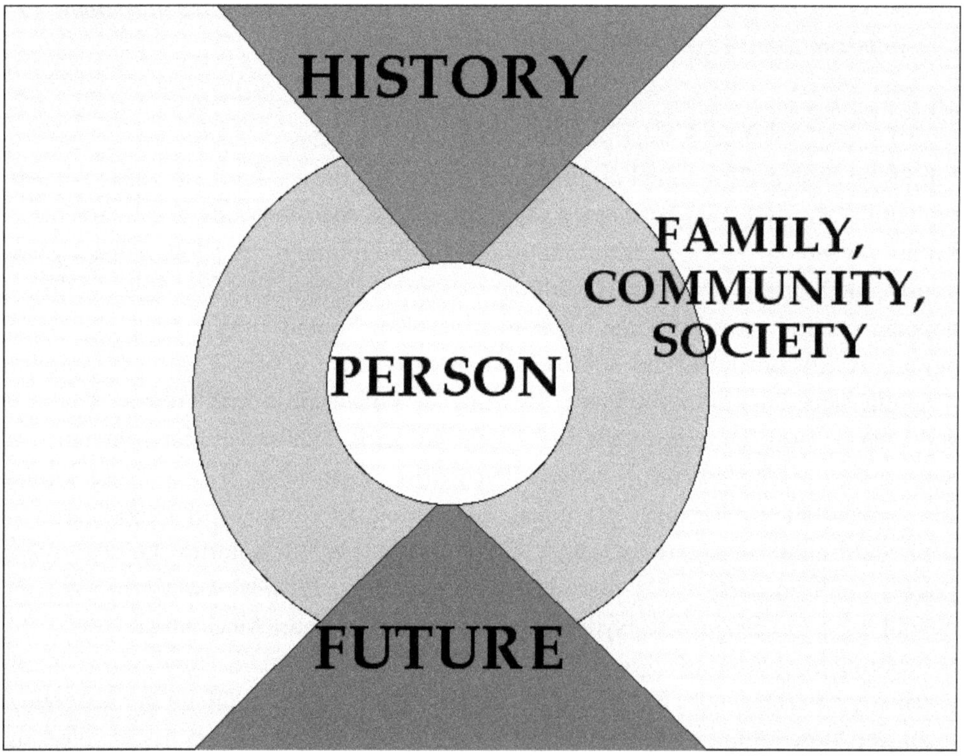

Figure 1: Context for Understanding People

will be discussed later, the family may stretch across borders and form transnational communities that intersect dominant and non-dominant societies. Clearly, such positionality increases the complexity of the lived experience of Chicano and Latino families.

Life Cycle Perspective

Family theorists McGoldrick, Carter, and Garcia Preto (2011) propose that families must be studied not only in terms of their social class, culture, and ethnicity but also with regard to the particular challenges presented by their individual and family stage of life. A life cycle perspective is utilized in this book because the strengths and challenges individuals and families face depend on their age and overall health (both individual and systemic). Such a perspective also considers the particular tasks families must negotiate as they transition from one stage of family life to another (Flores, Chicana and Chicano Mental Health 2013). These authors originally outlined stages of family formation beginning with coupling or marriage, followed by parenting (from babies through adolescents), and concluding with launching adult children. However, as European Americans began to postpone marriage and parenting, the authors added the stage of independence defined as single adults living apart from their parents. Likewise, as the "Baby Boomer" generation began to age, the stage of retirement or senior years was added (McGoldrick et al. 2005). Clearly, not all families follow a linear developmental path, and, among Latinos, leaving home or launching may not be a cultural ideal (as discussed below), and raising grandchildren or continuing to live in extended family households may be a common pattern. Although limited by differences based on social class and culture and ethnicity, the life cycle perspective sheds light on the challenges families may face at various points in their formation. Likewise, such a perspective takes into consideration how the stresses of daily living, economic problems, chronic illness, death of a family member, migration, separation or divorce, and, for Latina/os, unauthorized status and the threat of detection and deportation can disrupt the normative processes of family life.

Family theorists suggest that mastering the skills and milestones of each life cycle stage allows individuals within families, and the family system as a whole, to successfully move from one stage of development to the next. Conversely, failure to master the skills may result in relational difficulties and greater challenges in future transitions. Family life cycle theory suggests that successful transitioning may also help to prevent disease and emotional or stress-related disorders (McGoldrick et al. 2005). Others posit that difficulties or unsuccessful negotiation of life cycle stages may create patterns that are repeated invisibly or unconsciously across generations. For example, early or unplanned pregnancy resulting in a marriage may challenge the partners to solidify their couple relationship prior to raising children; additionally, it may contribute to subsequent separation or divorce if the couple was not able to build a solid foundation before facing the tasks of parenting small or adolescent offspring (Flores-Ortiz 1999; Flores 2005). Often, it is not until children are born that couples become aware of their expectations about each other in the rearing of children or of the cultural values that inform their parenting practices. If couples are unable to resolve their conflicts, the relationships may dissolve. Such a family pattern of divorce may be replicated in subsequent generations.

The caste/class system that evolved as a result of the conquest of the Americas and the subsequent miscegenation of the population also must be considered in trying to understand the marriage and partnering patterns of US Latinos and immigrants from the Americas. Of equal importance is the consideration of how adaptation to the US context and patterns of acculturation also may nuance the family life cycle of Latinos (Bernal 1984). In sum, to fully understand the ways in which Latinos form families it is crucial to be familiar with the socio-cultural and political context in which Latino families are embedded and the ways in which such context impacts the family's life cycle.

Latino Families: Structure and Functioning

Much has been written about Latino families from a sociological, anthropological, and psychological perspective. However, early writings tended to stereotype and overgeneralize from anecdotal or limited samples,[5] creating a unidimensional view of Mexican families, which was generalized to other Latino groups. Many early studies of Mexican families were conducted by European American researchers who had limited cultural knowledge of the groups under study. Such researchers also utilized the European American family as the norm to which Mexican and Chicano families were compared. The "idealized" Latino family that emerges in these studies is one that reflects a patriarchal structure wherein the male head of household reigns supreme and women are depicted as docile and submissive. In such families, males are socialized to be the providers and women the nurturers. While patriarchal arrangements are not unique to traditional families from collectivist cultures, early studies presented them as the prototype for Latino family organization. Latino families were often described as having rigid gender roles, to be hierarchical, and to privilege males over females. There was little discussion of how social class, generational status in the US, or other demographic factors could account for or influence such apparent family organization (Bernal 1984).

In his early writings, Salvador Minuchin argued that socioeconomically disadvantaged, multigenerational African American and Puerto Rican families should not be labeled dysfunctional simply because their family structure did not reflect the White, middle class ideal of a (heterosexual) couple with two children (Minuchin 1967). Instead, the difficulties these families faced were rooted in long-standing social and economic inequities. Solutions to their problems often could be found by supporting their culturally nuanced structure and organization; for example, grandmothers helping raise grandchildren so that women could work and help lift the family out of poverty.

It was not until the 1980s that more nuanced accounts of Latino family life began to emerge in the social science literature. For example, Norma Williams's (1990) study of Chicano families in Texas was the first book to address the changing patterns in the conjugal and familial patterns of this population, which resulted, in part, from women's increased participation in the labor market. Williams argued that traditional, patriarchal family arrangements were largely due to social class rather than a culturally based over-valuing of males and a devaluing of females. Moreover, she found that the type of work in which women engaged influenced their adherence to traditional gender roles. In her study, women who worked in the service industry or were blue-collar workers continued to view work as supplemental to their roles as mothers and wives, which remained their primary source of identity. Professional women evidenced a more complex identity. In addition, Williams found that working class women experienced less role strain than professional women, who tended to identify, first, as professional and, then, as wives or mothers. The rise of professional status among more educated Latinas and Chicanas contributed to relational tensions and psychological distress for many women. In my own study of Chicano families, I found that women who adhered to more traditional roles experienced more depression and anxiety than women who tried to balance their work and professional roles with their traditional roles. Yet, women who adhered to more traditional roles reported greater marital satisfaction than did professional women (Flores-Ortiz, Levels of Acculturation, Marital Satisfaction and Depression among Chicana Workers: a Psychological Perspective, 1993).

While many Latinos and Latinas may hold an idealized view of family life, social and economic realities, along with acculturation and the influence of modern life, may determine, in part, the structure of the families they ultimately form. As feminist family theorists have noted, expectations of women to fulfill spousal and maternal roles also will influence the negotiation of life cycle transitions in their and their family's life. Across the life cycle, Chicanas and Latinas are often expected to fulfill familial obligations that are gendered—daughter, friend, parent, spouse, cousin, *comadre*[6]—while men continue to be expected to be the primary economic support of the family. In more egalitarian relationships, women may expect (or demand) equal decision making and more collaborative parenting and home maintenance arrangements.

Elena Flores and colleagues (2004) examined the role of acculturation in the marital conflict experienced by Chicano couples. They found that with increased acculturation, Chicano couples tended to express their conflict openly and directly. Male partners often experienced their female partners to be more hostile or aggressive than their mothers had been. The men felt unprepared to respond to overt conflict. The women's behavior was described as a source of emotional distress to both partners and a potential threat to the viability of the relationship. Clearly, societal changes in the twentieth and twenty-first centuries have challenged couples to form families that can best support the individual and collective needs of their members. As indicated earlier, the family theory models discussed in this book are useful in understanding the contemporary challenges faced by Latino families while avoiding overgeneralizations that essentialize and stereotype the diverse Latino groups.

Relevant Political Issues

Central to understanding Latino family well-being is awareness of their position within the United States. A key aspect of Latino experience is the negotiation of its position as an ethnic minority and, in particular, the ways in which the government and other ethnocultural groups perceive and treat them. Many Mexican origin people who reside in the southwest are descendants of the original inhabitants of the United States who became foreigners and second-class citizens after the Mexican-American War and the Treaty of Guadalupe Hidalgo (Acuña 2010). Other Latino groups became US citizens after the US annexed Puerto Rico; yet others came to the US as exiles or refugees subsequent to the Cuban Revolution and the civil war in El Salvador. More recent Central and South American immigrants have come the US for a variety of political, educational, and social reasons. Mexican migration since 1848 has been largely work-related or for family reunification. The diverse roots of Latino migration and the long-standing presence of Mexicans in this country are unknown to many. Knowledge and awareness of this history is threatened by its exclusion from K–12 and post-secondary education, especially in states such as Arizona, which has banned the teaching of Chicano and other ethnic studies and books that document the experiences of Latinos in the US.

The US has a history of ambivalent immigration policies towards Latinos and Mexicans, in particular. During wars or economic booms, Mexicans have been sought or welcomed as guest workers (i.e., the Bracero program) only to be expelled when their labor was no longer needed or during economic downturns (Johnson 2009). No comprehensive immigration reform has taken place since the amnesty program passed by Congress and signed into law by President Reagan (the Immigration Reform and Control Act of 1986). This law legalized certain seasonal agricultural undocumented immigrants and adjusted the status of unauthorized immigrants who had entered the United States before January 1, 1982 and who had resided in the US continuously since then. Such persons had the penalty of a fine, had to pay back taxes, and had to admit guilt of unlawful entry. In addition, to qualify, immigrants were required to prove that they were not guilty of crimes, that they were in the country before January 1, 1982, and that they possessed minimal knowledge about US history, government, and the English language. About three million unauthorized immigrants were granted legal status through this act (Johnson 2004).

The Illegal Immigrant Reform and Immigrant Responsibility Act of 1996 (IIRIRA 96), passed by Congress and signed by President Clinton, pertained to the conditions by which certain unauthorized immigrants could adjust their status through "cancellation of removal" proceedings. The law also made the process more stringent. The war on terror, subsequent to the September 11, 2001 attacks in New York City, resulted in border protection policies that disproportionately targeted Mexicans and those crossing the southern border. The US Patriot Act, signed into law by President George W. Bush on October 26, 2001, expanded the offenses for which a person could be deported from the United States. Furthermore, immigration enforcement powers went beyond the scope of the federal government and expanded to the state and local governments, many of which have passed legislation outlawing many essential aspects of everyday lives for those who reside in the country without status, including Arizona's SB1070 and Alabama's HB56, among others.

In addition, deportations of unauthorized immigrants, many with long standing ties to the United States or who have US resident or citizen spouses and children, have resulted in the formation of transnational families as families are torn apart and children are separated from one or both parents. Such deportations and the threat of family separation also have contributed to significant psychological distress among mixed status families that remain in the US. [7] In 2008 alone, Immigration and Customs Enforcement apprehended 792,000 non-citizens, detained more than 397,000, and deported more than 259,000 of them (Dreby 2012). In the years 2010 and 2011, more than 400,000 people were deported from the United States each year. Of those individuals deported within the first six months, 46,000 had US citizen children who were either left behind or were forced to resettle in Mexico (Dreby 2012). These figures do not include the even greater number of individuals who returned to their home country through voluntary departure (476,000 in 2010 and 580,000 in 2009). According to Dreby, prior to the 9/11 attacks, only 189,000 immigrants were deported annually; these deportations were usually the result of felony convictions or engagement in other criminal activity. Given the failure of Congress to enact immigration reform during the Obama presidency, thousands of Latino families will continue to live under the threat of separation. The impact on children of living under such uncertainty has only recently begun to be studied (Crossroads 2012).

Thus, in addition to the micro- and macroaggressions Latinos experience due to their "minority status" in the United States, many Latinos also face discrimination based on the erroneous perception held by many that they are immigrants and likely unauthorized. The adverse consequences of discrimination on the physical health of Latinos and other people of color have been well documented (Flores 2013); the impact of such experiences on the family as a system is less documented in the family literature. In my 30 years of clinical practice as a family therapist, I have seen directly how such negative experiences impact the functioning and mental health of family members.

As McGoldrick has noted, how well a family is organized and how well it functions can only be fully understood if we examine it with consideration of the geopolitical structure within which it exists. Likewise, the family's socioeconomic position within society and the values, practices, and traditions of its members must be understood. These values, practices, and traditions evolve from the family's cultural influence(s) and spiritual and religious beliefs. All of these factors contribute to the diversity of family life and nuance both the strengths and challenges faced by contemporary families.

Organization of the Book

The writing of this book draws on my 40 years of experience as a master's-level family therapist and my 30 years of experience as a doctoral-level trained family theorist and therapist. Over the years, I have specialized in working with families and individuals affected by intergenerational trauma, which manifests as substance abuse and violence against the self and others as well as mood and anxiety disorders. I also have taught systems therapy to graduate students in professional schools and developed a course that offers psychological perspectives on Chicano and Latino families. This book was written by drawing on my experience teaching that course for 26 years in the department of Chicana and Chicano Studies at the University of California, Davis.

I am also an immigrant. My first migration occurred before I was one year of age when my Costa Rican-born father, who had migrated to Panama for work during the Second World War, decided to return to his country. My Panamanian mother became a coaxed migrant—she followed her husband to keep the family together. Eleven years later, my father decided to join his brothers in the United States. Once again, my mother followed my father "for my sake" so that I could grow up with both parents. I arrived in South Central Los Angeles on April 11, 1965, and experienced first hand, along with my nuclear family, much of what I write about in this book. My own family's migration narrative is used to highlight certain concepts. In addition, I incorporate case vignettes from my many years of practice to illustrate the challenges faced and successes attained by immigrant Latina/os and their US-raised-or-born offspring.

The book is divided into two parts; Part One consists of three chapters. The first chapter introduces the reader to the pioneering work of Celia Falicov, noted family psychologist, who developed the Multicultural Ecosystem Comparative Approach (MECA) (Falicov, Latino Families in Therapy, 1998 and 2014). Through the lenses of that model, I examine the social and cultural context of Latino and Chicano families. Chapter 2 foregrounds the influence of class, race, nativity, gender, and generational level on family structure and functioning, paying particular attention to the challenges of raising mixed race, bi- or multicultural children. Chapter 3 utilizes family systems theory and particular approaches (Contextual/Intergenerational, Narrative, and Just Theories) to investigate what constitutes a healthy, well-functioning Latino family. Through the use of case vignettes, examples of diverse family structures are examined; they include blended, remarried, and single-parent families, as well as families led by lesbian and gay parents. Readers are encouraged to examine their own families through the use of genealogy.

In the second part of the book, the challenges faced by Latino families are examined as well as the impact of intergenerational trauma on the lives of Latinos. Chapter 4 begins with an examination of troublesome triangles and continues with understanding the myriad factors that result in substance misuse and abuse, family violence, including child maltreatment, domestic violence, and sexual abuse. Chapter 5 offers an in-depth analysis on the impact of politics and policies on the formation of transnational families. Case vignettes are used to use to illustrate the challenges faced by mixed status families and families torn apart by deportation. Chapter 6 offers psycho-educational strategies to heal and transform hurtful ways of being into supportive, culturally rooted relational patterns in family life. The book concludes with a discussion of the challenges that continue to face Latino families and offers community-based participatory action research strategies to promote family justice and well-being among rural and urban Latino families.

Intended Audience

While this book has been developed for undergraduate instruction, it also can be useful for graduate students and professionals in education, psychology, social work, and related fields who wish to increase their cultural humility[8] in their work with diverse Latino families. While the book does not provide a comprehensive review of all family theories that may be helpful to understand and support Latino families, it provides a perspective rooted in respect for the diversity and complexity of Latino families in the twenty-first century. This is not a handbook on "how to do therapy or treat Latinos;" however, knowledge of and sensitivity to the issues addressed in the book are essential elements for evidence-based therapy with Latino families (G. Bernal 2012).

This book is written with the hope that it can contribute to increased justice and fairness towards all families irrespective of race, class, ethnicity, nativity, sexuality, or status by addressing the intersectionalities that nuance family formation and functioning.

PART ONE

CHAPTER 1

LATINO FAMILIES IN CONTEXT

> *As a nation of immigrants, the United States has always faced the challenge of understanding and integrating racial and ethnic diversity. This challenge has never been greater than now* (Falicov, Latino Families in Therapy: A guide to multicultural practice 1998, 5).

Latino families in the United States constitute an ethnic/racial/cultural mosaic that reflects the multiple migrations of Europeans to the American Continent as well as the cultural exchange between pre-Colombian cultures and those of Asia and Africa. Likewise, the more recent migrations of Latinos from South, Central, and North America and intermarriage with other racial and ethnic groups have led to a US-based Latino population that is racially and ethnically diverse.

While the US Census categorizes Latinos as either White or Black, the majority of Latinos in the United States are *mestizos* (Spanish and Amerindian) and have historical connection to Africans, Asians, and Middle Eastern people. According to noted author and diplomat Carlos Fuentes (Fuentes 1993), to understand contemporary Latinos one needs to comprehend the multicultural and multiracial context of Spain at the time of the conquest and the already complex ethnic/racial world of indigenous America. Race and ethnicity are interwoven into the identity of Latinos. Moreover, due to the caste and class system that evolved in the Americas post-conquest, race and color have complicated the identify formation of Latinos as well as their family relations; oftentimes, family members may be privileged or problematized because of their skin color or phenotype (Quintana 2009). [9]

The largest Latino group in the United States is of Mexican origin either by nativity or migration. However, the twentieth century saw large migrations of individuals and families from Cuba, El Salvador, Honduras, Argentina, Colombia, and Venezuela (US Census 2010). These migrations were largely the result of political instability or economic crisis in the country of origin. The influx of other immigrant groups from Latin America has resulted in a more complex national identity for the children of immigrants who intermarry or partner with individuals from different national origins. Furthermore, while many US-born-or-raised Latinos may use a term that implies ethnic/racial/cultural homogeneity, such as Latino or Hispanic, most Latinos continue to identify with their national origins or those of their parents (Bernal 1984) or choose identifiers that further nuance their ethnic and racial complexity, such as Blackxican, to refer to African American and Mexican parentage (Flores 2006).

To fully understand the context of Latino families in the US necessitates inquiring about their national origins, ethnic identification, generational status in the US[10], and various other factors that nuance the context and experience of Latinos, particularly their ecological niche within the larger US society, the family's journey of migration and culture change, and their family organization and life cycle. Without such an extensive analysis, the diversity of the Latino experience cannot be fully grasped.

THE MULTICULTURAL ECOSYSTEMIC COMPARATIVE APPROACH [MECA]

Developed by Psychologist Celia Falicov in the 1980s as a result of her own experiences as an immigrant to the US and as a psychologist treating Latino families and individuals from diverse origins, the MECA model offers a culturally sensitive approach to understanding the lived experience of and the challenges faced by these families. Falicov argues that focusing exclusively on a group's "cultural context" can essentialize, oversimplify, and lead to erroneous and stereotypic depictions of a group. A multicultural perspective, in contrast, recognizes the complexity of Latinos' experience and identities. By Ecosystemic, Falicov refers to the "unique combination of multiple contexts and partial perspectives that defines each family's culture" (Falicov 1998, 15). She refers to these contexts and perspectives as the family's ecological niche.

Falicov offers four generic domains of analysis in her model; the first addresses the journey of migration and the culture changes that result from migration. The second, the ecological context, examines "diversity in where and how the family lives and fits in the broader environment" (Falicov 1988, 17), paying particular attention to the intersectionalities of Latino experience, the race, ethnicity, class, religious, spiritual and educational communities within which families live and interact. This dimension also examines the explanatory models of health and illness held by diverse Latino groups. The third generic domain examines the family organizations of Latinos and how cultural values influence diverse family formations. Lastly, the fourth domain focuses on the life cycle of families and how the family's culture patterns influence developmental milestones.

> *The process of leaving one's home country and encountering a new one constitutes an overlapping of events, developmental changes, and existential tasks that render a "very unique phenomenology of migration" (Falicov 1989, 46).*

Journey of Migration and Culture Change

Latinos exist as a result of the contact of distinct cultural groups at the time of the conquest. Thus, migration is not only central to the psyche of Latinos but is a key factor in how family life is constituted regardless of whether the migration occurred yesterday or many generations before. Migration is a process of relocation that includes both a physical and psychological experience. Latinos share many similarities with US immigrants from other parts of the world in terms of the process of migration but often diverge in terms of the reception or degree of welcoming experienced from the host or dominant cultures.

Falicov proposes that both sociological and psychological adaptation post-migration is influenced by the "changes in meaning" systems. She utilized the metaphor of rooting and uprooting to describe these changes in meaning in response to physical, social, and cultural uprooting. She describes physical uprooting as learning to live without the familiar sounds and sights, smells, and faces of home. When my parents migrated from Panama to Costa Rica, I missed the sound of the ocean as I fell asleep; I longed for the smell of the Caribbean, the gentle breeze of the ocean air. I had no recollection of the place of my birth after my first migration at one year of age. But my senses remembered—and missed—the physical geography of the town where I was born. These memories returned in dreams in my adulthood after having migrated north once again even farther from the place of my birth (Flores-Ortiz, *My Father's Hands*, 2001).

The extent to which immigrants can recreate home in the new context or find elements of home will facilitate their adaptation. For many immigrant Latinos, being able to cook familiar foods is essential; not finding the necessary ingredients to do so may trigger a crisis. Living in the San Fernando Valley of California in the late 1960s before the Latino population grew in significant numbers, my father had to drive my mother to East Los Angeles so she could find the roots, vegetables, and cuts of meat with which she was familiar and the butchers and produce vendors who could speak to her in Spanish. Having left her older children and extended family behind in her native Panama, my mother clung to her language and familiar foods as her life raft. Her Sunday dinners consisted of *arroz con guandules, ropa vieja, patacones* or *platanos fritos*[11]. She kept Panama alive through her cooking. My second-generation Honduran son-in-law prepares traditional Afro-Caribbean Honduran dishes his parents taught him to cook. His wife, my daughter, cooks Mexican, Panamanian, Costa Rican, Honduran, and Tex-Mex foods with the same ease she prepares pasta and hamburgers. At various times on any given week, the sounds and smells of my current home transport me back to the "home" where my spirit feels most at ease. Many immigrant Latinos live in two or more psychological spaces; their offspring sometimes feel that they don't belong; they are neither "here" nor "there" but, instead, inhabit "cultural borderlands" or the interstices of cultures (Anzaldua 1987; Falicov 1989). Such psychological homelessness (Hardy and Laszloffy 2005) can adversely impact both their own emotional well-being and that of the families they form.

In addition to physical uprooting, Falicov also notes that social uprooting "compounds the sense of physical alienation and intrapsychic confusion" (Falicov 1998, 53) resulting from migration. Social marginality and social isolation, which many immigrants face, exacerbates such distress and may evolve into mental-health problems of anxiety and depression (Flores 2013) as well as impact the US-born children, particularly if the family's economic status results in settlement in under-resourced communities ridden with crime and despair where education is poor and upward mobility is difficult to attain. In addition to recreating home through foods, decorations, and so on, immigrants often need to have contact with co-nationals, listen to news "from home," watch TV programs, and engage in activities that were performed in their country, such as playing soccer, *ballet folklorico*, religious festivals, and national holidays. Immigrants may also introduce their children to these practices to minimize the impact of the social uprooting.

In my family, when I was growing up, the women gathered for coffee and gossip every afternoon at three. Since my migration to the US at age 13, I have missed being part of that ritual and find the afternoon a time of longing where I need to spend quiet time and have caffeine. After 50 years in the United States, I still feel the impact of the physical and social uprooting caused by my parents' migration to the US. As my mother aged and after my father died, she longed to return to die in her homeland. I granted her that wish ... stirring up more feelings in me of social and physical uprooting: my mother and father had been the links and anchors to my geographic past. As discussed later, painful events, such as the loss of a family member at particular stages of the family life cycle, may lead to emotional distress or family crisis as the wounds caused by migration are reopened.

Immigrants often arrive with a preconception of what the new country will offer. Sometimes the "American Dream," the belief that economic prosperity will be easier to attain in the US and that adaptation will not be so difficult, influences these expectations. The reality of life in the US may lead to disappointment and result in crisis, which can manifest as anxiety or depression (Falicov 1989; Flores 2013; Sluzki 1979). Such cultural uprooting may also lead to family polarization as children grow up and become socialized in a bi- or multicultural context as a result of exposure to other cultures (Falicov 1989). Parents may fear that their children will be lost to them if they acculturate too much to the US ways of being (Flores, Parenting 2005).

According to Falicov, immigrants create a story of their migration, a migration narrative that helps them maintain psychological and cultural continuity and gives meaning to their experience in the new social context. These narratives often influence how family life is organized and how the family story and the cultural values of the parents are transmitted to the young. As a result, understanding the impact of migration on the family by its members as well as professionals who work with families (teachers, psychologists, social workers, etc.) is facilitated by eliciting the family's migration narrative.

Another Argentinian family theorist, psychiatrist Carlos Sluzki, offered a model to understand how family dysfunction can develop by analyzing the process of migration of any given family. Sluzki proposes that migration entails stages with concomitant challenges and crises. There are five stages: the first is the preparatory stage; the second entails the actual migration; the third is the period of overcompensation; the fourth deals with the decompensation or crisis; and the fifth and last addresses the intergenerational phenomena that can affect future generations.

Preparatory Stage

Key considerations in the preparatory stage include the degree of planning prior to migration. Part of the analysis entails determining who decided that a migration would occur, the reasons for it, who is chosen to stay behind, and how the decisions are communicated—or not—to members of the family. This is often the time when particular roles are assigned to family members. Clearly, the extent to which there is preparation, information about the receiving community, and possibilities of employment will largely influence how the other stages of migration are experienced or negotiated.

Actual Migration

The family narrative often provides an account of what happened during the migration, with details of how the journey began, how long it lasted, and who helped along the way. The movie "My Family/*Mi Familia*"[12] provides the story of a young, rural Mexican immigrant, Jose Sanchez, and his journey north, as well as the fate of his US-born children and wife. In the movie, upon arrival to the US, Jose tells the only person who might know of him that he walked all the way from central Mexico to East Los Angeles. He creates a narrative full of adventure that was part myth, part reality. Many immigrants, particularly those from Mexico and Central America, often face unspeakable horrors, trauma, and even death in their efforts to enter the US without inspection[13]. Such histories often result in secrets and silences meant to spare future generations the burden of suffering experienced by the immigrants. Shame of one's origins and of unauthorized border crossings may also lead to the creation of alternative stories that hide elements of the actual migration. However, as will be discussed in later chapters, such silences and secrets may appear in subsequent generations as legacies and invisible loyalties (Boszormenyi-Nagy 1984).

Period of Overcompensation

The first few weeks and months after migration are characterized by the immigrants' efforts to settle and survive. The primary tasks consist of instrumental activities: finding work, housing, schools. The central focus is on survival and resettlement. There is generally a moratorium on feelings as these may interfere with the tasks necessary to settle and reorganize life in a new context. The extent to which the immigrant has family or social networks that support it during this stage, the easier it will be to settle. However, many immigrants spend decades trying to root themselves and become economically sound. They may not be able (or willing) to send for family members and, thus, create de facto transnational families. In particular, those who work seasonally in agriculture as day laborers or in the service sector or construction may only earn enough to subsist and send remittances to their family "back home." Eventually, however, for all immigrants, a period of decompensation or crisis will occur.

Period of Decompensation or Crisis

When his wife, Maria, a US citizen, is deported as a result of a workplace raid, Jose Sanchez is left to care for his young son and daughter with only the help of his long-lost relative, *El Californio*. This begins a personal process of decompensation for Jose and sets the stage for a family crisis that will continue for generations. His second son, Chucho, is born in Mexico and nearly drowns during his mother's efforts to return home. Chucho personifies the child of immigrants who rejects both his parents' culture and that of the dominant culture that rejects him. Chucho becomes the identified patient in his family, the child who embodies the conflicts of biculturality and resorts to delinquent and self-injurious behaviors to call attention to the family losses and the failure of the American dream. To understand family dysfunction, which will be discussed in greater detail in later chapters, it is important to clarify when the period of decompensation began for a family, what triggered it, how long it has lasted, and who in the family has become the mourner, the underaculturator, the one whose behavior calls attention to losses related to migration. Many families spend years and, in some cases, multiple generations in a state of crisis. Open recognition of the changes in meaning systems that led to the crisis and uncovering the migration narrative can be a beginning step in healing the family's spiritual and emotional wounds in the second and third generation and beyond.

Transgenerational Phenomena

Sluzki posits that the issues not resolved by the migrating generation will be manifested in the children. As did Chucho in *Mi Familia*, some second- or third-generation offspring of immigrants will reject the culture of the parents and the values that to them seem antiquated or not useful in the US context. These cultural cut-offs may, in turn, result in feelings of marginality, substance misuse, and other forms of individual and family problems (Cervantes 2004). In addition, intergenerational and/or gender conflicts may ensue as some family members with greater exposure to the dominant culture(s) may acculturate at a much faster rate and appear to shift their loyalty to the US rather than the country of origin. Women may enter the labor force and develop their own economic viability; thereby, a shift in power relations may occur in their relationships that can threaten males who hold more traditional values (Flores-Ortiz, *Voices from the Couch: the Co-Construction of a Chicana Psychology*, 1997). Individuals within families may experience difficulties in making commitments (jobs, schools, relationships), particularly if the immigrant parents maintained the dream of returning to the country of origin and did not support the cultural adaptation of their offspring to the US. Often, these children of immigrants describe their lives as waiting for a return to somewhere unknown or unfamiliar to them, which precluded their setting roots in the country of their birth. As they say, "*no somos ni de aqui, ni de alla*" (we are neither from here nor from there) (Flores 2013).

What Sluzki posits and many mental health professionals observe is that migration-related legacies, whether historical or contemporary, may transform into family dysfunction(s). In addition, according to family theory scholars (Falicov 1989; Sluzki 1979), the subsequent adaptation of individuals and families will partly depend on whether the migration was forced (that is, in response to political, social, or natural crises), coaxed (as when one spouse follows the other who migrated previously or when children migrate to join their parents), or voluntary. In the latter, the departure is fueled by a desire to seek better economic opportunities or adventure or to follow a historical legacy of migration. Furthermore, within families, roles are assigned pre- and post-migration. Such role assignment may be somewhat unconscious or invisible to the family. Initially, these roles may serve an adaptive function for the family, but, over time, they may contribute to dysfunction or individual and family distress.

Sluzki identifies four roles commonly assigned in immigrant families pre- and post-migration; the **bridge**, the **mourner**, the **under-acculturator**, and the **over-acculturator**. For example, a family member or friend who migrated previously may become the **bridge** for subsequent migrations. This individual may become the hero or villain of the migration narrative; he or she can be blamed for later family problems or credited for the family success. A family may have more than one bridge, or various members may become bridges to others at various points in the family life cycle. Sometimes, children of immigrants become bridges by connecting the family to the US or back to the country of origin as is the case with children or grandchildren of Cuban immigrants who have reconnected to Cuba.[14] In *Mi Familia*, Toni, one of Jose and Maria's daughters, becomes a nun; she later leaves the convent and becomes an immigrants' rights activist. In her own way, she becomes a bridge that connects the past and the present of the Sanchez family.

In my own family, a paternal uncle left home as a young man to seek adventure in Venezuela as well as to leave a conflicted relationship with his father. From Venezuela, he went to the United States. Many years later, he returned to Costa Rica with pockets full of dollars and tales about life in Hollywood. Within a few months, most of the young men in my neighborhood had left for the United States. This uncle encouraged and finally convinced my father to migrate to Los Angeles, California, as well. This uncle was my family's bridge to the United States.

The **mourners** in a family are expected to remain connected to the country of origin. They may be expected to hold the memories, write letters, contact the family left behind, or maintain cultural ties, continuing to speak the language and embody the culture in some way. These family members, such as Jose's daughter in *Mi Familia*, who owned a Mexican restaurant and nurtured everyone with food, keep the culture of origin alive although, sometimes, in frozen ways[15] (Flores-Ortiz, La Mujer y la Violence: a Culturally Based Model for the Understanding and Treatment of Domestic Violence in Chicano and Latino Families, 1993). Very often, the mourner in the immigrant generation will be female. Over time, she may be frozen into the role and become symptomatic (experience depression, for example).

The **under-acculturator** is the US-born-or-raised child of immigrants who is also expected to remain loyal to the culture of origin. Often, this entails rejecting the new cultural context. If this occurs, he or she is less likely to have a successful adaptation and may experience marginalization from both cultures as did Chucho, first, and, then, Jimmy in *Mi Familia*. In the second generation, under-acculturators may become challenged by alcohol and other drug abuse or delinquency (Cervantes 2004). Other family members may hold ambivalent feelings toward them: admiration, if they maintain cultural ties, shame, if they are not "making it" in the new cultural milieu. As do the mourners in immigrant families, the under-acculturators embody the unresolved issues of the immigrants and through their dysfunction or suffering, remind the family of the losses endured or resulting from the migration.

Every immigrant family may have several bridges, mourners, and under-acculturators. The same individual may shift roles over the family life cycle. While mourners and under-acculturators may preserve directly or indirectly the family's ties to the ancestral culture, the **over-acculturator** is expected to actualize the family's "American dream." He or she often becomes the interpreter of the culture and translator of language for the family. Generally, it is the older child who occupies this role. In some families, it is the youngest child who attempts to actualize the dream." In *Mi Familia*, Paco, the narrator, and Bill (who was baptized Guillermo but Anglicized his name to minimize his Mexicanness) occupy these roles. Paco does this while maintaining a bicultural identity; Bill tries to assimilate and appears ashamed of his Mexican roots. As is the case with under-acculturators, the family may hold ambivalent feelings of both pride and shame towards them; some may call them *vendido/as* (sellouts or whitewashed).

The MECA model also sheds light on the challenges of children of immigrants by underscoring the importance of understanding the processes of acculturation, transculturation, hybridity, and biculturality.

Acculturation

This is a controversial and extensively studied construct, which refers to an individual or group's ability to adapt to the new context and adopt cultural values, ideals, traditions, and practices while retaining aspects of the culture of origin. The process is multidimensional and situational and depends on the degree of cultural and social capital the immigrant family can provide its members (Padilla 1980). Family members who speak English and have higher education will have an easier time adjusting to the US context, finding work, and/or continuing with their education than those who do not know the language or have employment skills that are not highly valued by US society, such as agricultural work. Research findings suggest (Cuellar 2004) that behaviors, attitudes, and practices acculturate at a faster rate than values and traditions with resulting dissonance between behaviors and underlying values. Moreover, core values, such as *familismo*, may not acculturate while others adapt to new environment.

In studying the level of acculturation of a family and its influence on family structure and functioning, it is important to distinguish between *cultural ideals and cultural realities.* While a couple may desire to create a traditional family in which the woman stays home to raise her children (cultural ideal), the economic and social reality they face demands that both partners work. The cultural reality may create distress for the couple as they encounter dissonance between the cultural ideal and their inability to fulfill it. Such distress can be compounded if the extended family and the larger society do not support the idea and reality of working mothers or devalue their contributions. It is common for family members to have different levels of acculturation, which can also contribute to conflict and misunderstanding within and across generations of the same family. It is also common for families to become more traditional as they get older or at particular points in the family life cycle. For example, Chicano parents may adopt a permissive parenting style when their children are young in order to foster independence, free will, and warmer relationships with their children than they had with their own, more authoritarian parents. However, as their children enter adolescence, the parents may fall back on more authoritative discipline to counter the "over-permissiveness" they see in their youngsters' behavior, which the parents may begin to label as lack of respect. This can be very confusing to the children and distressing to all involved. Therefore, in studying acculturation, it is important to examine what changes in families and what stays the same both in terms of ideals and realities. While attitudes and behaviors may become more modern, core values may remain fairly traditional.[16]

In contrast to acculturation, **assimilation** requires acceptance by the "host" or dominant culture; thus, English-speaking, fair-skinned Latinos may have an easier time being accepted by other groups in the US than more indigenous-looking or darker-skinned Latinos. In their efforts to assimilate, to "try to pass" for Anglos by changing their name or identifying with a "Spanish" identity, individuals or groups make efforts to surrender their psychological loyalty and adherence to the culture of origin and join the new culture. Individuals who are similar to the dominant group (in terms of race, class, language, culture, religion, politics, etc.) are more likely to assimilate. In *Mi Familia*, Guillermo, despite his phenotype, attempts to assimilate by changing his name to Bill, speaking English, and planning to marry a European American woman. As a college educated attorney, he tries to fit in by downplaying his Mexicanness. Sometimes, such efforts are the result of the discrimination individuals face due to their ethnic or racial identity (Falicov 1989). Many Mexican Americans who grew up in the 1940s and 1950s intentionally did not teach their children Spanish to protect them from the pervasive discrimination Mexican origin people experienced in the southwestern United States. Many of the children and grandchildren of these Mexican Americans, in turn, participated and provided leadership in the Chicano Movement of the 1960s, which called attention to and worked to rectify the injustices faced by previous generations (Zavella 2001).

It is important to keep in mind that acculturation and assimilation are distinct processes and that assimilation is not the end result of acculturation. Both are strategies for survival among immigrants and for developing a sense of belonging for the children of immigrants.

LaFramboise (1993), among other theorists, points to the limitations of linear models of cultural adaption and suggests, instead, alternation models, which posit that individuals can have a sense of belonging in two cultures without compromising their sense of belonging to either (Falicov 1989). Individuals can be bicultural when they alternate or integrate two languages or cultures. These individuals may utilize different cultural values, perform behavior, and reflect attitudes of either or both cultures, depending on the social context, life stage, and so on. Bicultural individuals tend to function equally well in both cultures, unlike monocultural individuals who function best in only one context or marginalized individuals who function well in neither, such as Chucho in *Mi Familia,* for example.

Hybridization

Hybridization refers to the blending rather than alternating of cultural meanings that is often seen among children of immigrants. According to Falicov (1989), hybridization may "occur in cultural situations in which traditions are not quite past and modernity is not yet wholly present" (74). This process implies a " sort of cognitive cultural know-how" of knowing intuitively or learning with purpose when a particular cultural code is appropriate to one setting versus another. For example, a highly educated woman who is assertive at work and who demands egalitarianism in her intimate relationships may become more solicitous and deferential when interacting with her immigrant parents or grandparents. Hybrid families may have a larger cultural repertoire to respond to dilemmas of family life than families that adhere strictly to traditional values or who, in their efforts to assimilate, try to divest themselves of the values of the culture of origin (Falicov 1989).

Transculturation

Here, we recognize that cultural adaptation is not a linear process. Individuals and families may cross borders linguistically, psychologically, and physically. This may be easier for some Latinos groups, such as Puerto Ricans, who are already US citizens, and Mexicans, who have geographic proximity to Mexico. Individuals and families often navigate multiple cultural spaces. Moreover, what baggage migrants bring along and leave behind has implications for post-migration adjustment. What comes in the luggage (factual and imaginary), the cultural and social capital of a migrant, often determines their ability to acculturate or transculturate. For US-born-or-raised offspring, cultural alternation may be necessary. For some, the ability to cross-linguistic and literal borders is essential for sound mental health. When families experience conflict, it is helpful to assess to what extent acculturation, transculturation, or alternating cultural practices may be present and how they contribute to the family distress. Likewise, within these practices, solutions to family dilemmas may be found (Falicov 1998).

In summary, migrations are massive ecological transitions in time and space that may be filled with loss and disarray, resulting in long-term implications for the migrants and future generations. Involuntary, forced, or coerced migrations may increase vulnerabilities to physical and mental distress as well as family dysfunction. However, migration also creates opportunities for change and adaptation. The family's migration narrative may elucidate the sources of resilience in the family as well as the origins of present day problems.

Ecological Context

Among the various Latino groups, similarities may exist in terms of language, cultural values, and religion; however, differences also may exist depending on country of origin, reason for migration, and US social and political attitudes towards their particular group, as well as the value and cultural changes that accompany migration. Rumbaut (1994) offers a model of segmented adaptation that is helpful in understanding how migration and its sequelae affect family life. He argues that adjustment to a new context is not a unilinear or unidirectional process. Instead, his theory focuses on three issues when seeking to understand where immigrants settle and how well they fare: first, the nature of migration to the host country (forced or voluntary); second, the initial resources that immigrants bring (education and job skills, social networks); and third, the social context that greets immigrants in the host culture (positive, negative, or ambivalent) (Portes and Borocz 1989, 614–620). For example, early waves of Cuban immigrants who were fleeing the Cuban revolution were generally welcomed to the US and afforded exile status, which included government assistance to reestablish themselves. These Cubans were mostly educated, White, and members of the professional classes. In contrast, exiles who came in the late 1980s through the Mariel Boatlift were less educated, younger, and about 20% were Black. *Marielitos*, as other Cubans and Latinos named them, who did not have family members in the US who could vouch for them, faced detention for many months and many ultimately became part of the Cuban underclass of South Florida. Others adjusted and integrated into the larger Cuban community (Skop 2001).

From a sociological perspective, three factors are critical to immigrant adjustment; essential among these is the cultural and social capital an immigrant brings; the more resources an immigrant has, such as high level of education and occupational skills, the more she or he will be able to meet the challenges encountered post-migration. A second factor is the variety and kind of government programs available to immigrants or what Portes and Borocz (1989) term "the context of reception" by the host government. These are also key to the adjustment process. In the case of the first wave of Cuban immigrants of the 1950s, the support included financial assistance and educational programs (Skop 2001). This level of government reception, as Skop has noted, is quite distinct from the minimal assistance offered to labor migrants. Instead, these are often demonized, criminalized, and blamed for the economic problems in the US. A third factor that predicts the immigrants' structural integration is the degree of solidarity and sense of community with compatriots already in the US. Clearly, family and social networks will also facilitate immigrant adjustments. As has been evident in the increased anti-immigrant sentiments of the late twentieth century, not all established Mexican American or Latino compatriots are welcoming of newer, unauthorized immigrants from Central America or Mexico. In fact, many politically conservative Latino groups argue against immigration reform and endorse stricter border enforcement (Southern Poverty Law Center 2014).

Skop proposes that "place of incorporation" is a fourth element necessary in the segmented adaptation framework. Where immigrants ultimately settle may reflect the degree of socio-cultural and economic incorporation of the particular group. Many scholars argue that ethnicity and ethnic identification may exert some influence in residential location. Ethnic enclaves remain, but many Latinos live in integrated neighborhoods in urban, suburban, and rural areas of the United States. Although two decades ago most Latinos lived in rural or semirural communities, since the 2000 census, Latinos are predominantly urban dwellers. Moreover, Skop argues that ethnic communities may be symbolically constructed and not necessarily located within a particular geographic space. For example, Mexican immigrants from Michoacán may continue to identify with their *Michoacano* roots and town of origin despite living in racially and ethnically integrated urban centers in the US. While their identity is nuanced by US experience, they may remain connected psychologically to their "hometown;" they may evidence transcultural or hybrid cultural practices. Such identification may continue into the second and third generation, even when US-born children have not ever lived or visited their parents' or grandparents' *rancho* or town.

In summary, Latino families in the United States vary according to socio-economic status, geographical location, and country of origin. The journey of migration and culture change as well as the degree of structural integration of immigrant groups has implications for Latino family organization.

Family Organization

As suggested by sociologists, family structure is often determined by location, work, (migrant, seasonal, blue, white collar, professional) and kinship or social ties that were pre-existent to the migration. The basic social unit idealized by many Latinos is the extended family, which may include three or four generations as well as horizontal relationships among siblings and cousins (even twice or thrice removed) (Falicov 1989). Such preferences reflect the core value of *familismo* (familism), defined as a strong orientation and commitment toward the family. *Familismo* is not intrinsic to Latino families; rather, it is characteristic of collectivist cultures[17]. *Familismo* is also connected to a high value on (heterosexual) marriage, childbearing, and responsibility toward siblings. *Familismo* is also accompanied with prescribed duties, including loyalty and interconnection to family members in both the nuclear and extended family. The ideology of *familismo* extends beyond blood relations to include fictive kin (individuals not related by blood but who have the status of family), which may include extended families of several generations and godparents (*compadres*), in-laws, and close friends (Falicov, 1989; Flores, *Parenting* 2005).

While the cultural ideal reflects the collectivist value of an extended, close-knit, and interdependent family organization, post-migration realities result in more diverse family structures. In many cases, the ideal of an extended family system has been replaced by single parent families, nuclear family households, and "alternative families" (e.g., single adults living together, gay and lesbian couples, common-law arrangements, and several families living together to share costs) (Flores 2005). As Minuchin argued several decades ago, the organization of a family must be understood in terms of the factors that help shape it, in particular, the economic realities of the family. Likewise, nativity, generational status, and the social position of the family may influence its structure and organization[18].

As Falicov (1998) points out, regardless of the household composition, a central organizing principle of Latino families is the concept of connectedness and the importance ascribed to family bonds. Such connectedness is evident in family rituals, such as baptisms, *quinceañeras*[19] and other family gatherings. In addition, families who espouse *familismo* expect frequent contact through visits or phone calls to parents, elders in the family, and godparents. Participation in family events and gatherings is valued and expected, as well. The failure to meet such expectations due to migration or economic realities that preclude leisure time activities can be a source of family conflict. In my own extended family, a great deal of resentment was built because I could not attend family gatherings "when I was away at school." After some time, I was no longer invited to baby showers or the birthday parties of my cousin's children. The assumption was that I was "too busy for family affairs." On more than one occasion, my parents were expressed sympathy for their lot—having a highly educated professional daughter—which, in their eyes, changed me. I was seen as no longer prioritizing family activities. As will be discussed in later chapters, the appearance that family connection is not as important as *it should be* for children of immigrants can be a source of distress and conflict for both parents and adult children.

The value of family connection is transmitted to family members by modeling devotion to parents, particularly in their older years, participation in family rituals, and by inculcating in the children another important value for Latinos—*personalismo*—which is defined as the concern for the well-being of others and the ethical stance that conflict should be avoided to save face and maintain harmony in family relations. The central element of *personalismo* is emotional resonance and personal involvement with family encounters (Falicov 1998). These values are related to the concept of familial self, a sense of self that includes one's close relationships as part of who one is (Falicov 1989, 163). *Tu eres mi otro yo* (you are my other self) is an indigenous Meso American value commonly held among Chicanas and Chicanos of varying generations (Tello 2008). This value reflects the notion of the familial self. Another saying in Spanish, *hoy por ti, mañana por mi,* also illustrates this concept. Inherent in the belief that "today I do for you because tomorrow you will do for me" is the value of interconnectedness and the reciprocity that is expected in family relationships. The familial self is balanced by the private self, which may be more bounded and more difficult to access in order to maintain relational order. Highly familistic individuals may keep their feelings to themselves and avoid direct confrontations or direct expression of disagreement to protect the feelings of the other and, thereby, maintain harmony. The feelings may be expressed indirectly or shared with a third party who can try to convey the information without hurting the feelings of the person responsible for the concerns of the aggrieved. Such style of communication may become problematic when family members of different generations or partners from different cultural backgrounds or levels of acculturation do not share the "cultural rules" that govern such interactions.

When US-raised-or-born children appear to prioritize their private self over the familial self, the immigrant parents may perceive their children as disrespectful, uncaring, or selfish. When one of my therapy clients, an immigrant woman from Nicaragua, told her mother that she was not willing to expose her daughter to her stepfather's drinking and verbal abusiveness, her mother cried in despair, "you don't love me; you are going to kill me with your selfishness." Although the client understood how her mother would interpret her boundary setting as uncaring, she still felt the hurt of her mother's words and experienced significant guilt. Although this interaction is reflective of problematic family dynamics (which will be described in later chapters), it also highlights the differences that emerge between generations in how *personalismo* and *familismo* are lived and negotiated between first- and second-generation Chicanas and Chicanos, Latinas and Latinos.

Since Latinos often inhabit two psychological spaces (US and country of origin), their family structure and organization may reflect hybridity or different cultural patterns at various points in the life cycle. For example, a young couple may want to live independently of their parents. When a child is born, they may wish to live in closer proximity to their parents for emotional and logistical support. The grandparents may expect to be very involved with the grandchildren and may suffer if distance or conflict separates them. Latino adults are expected to take care of aging parents; inability to do so will cause significant emotional distress. Families that adhere to the traditional value of interconnectedness will often rally around family members in need to provide emotional, financial, or logistical support and, thereby, reduce stress or the burden of caregiving (Flores, *Embodying Dimentia: Remembrances of Memory Loss* 2008).

Given the diversity of Latinos, it is important to determine how cultural values, their socioeconomic status, nativity, and generation have influenced and shaped their family structure and organization. Equally important is the recognition that the ecological niche occupied by Latinos may be different across generations, as some family members may experience upward mobility through education, work, or marriage, while others may not and, yet, may face greater economic stress and poverty than did the immigrant generation. Another important aspect to consider is the family life cycle.

Family Life Cycle

From a developmental perspective, families are systems that evolve over time. Families, like individuals, go through stages of development. The family life cycle is based on the assumption that individuals continue to marry and form nuclear families. However, it is important to consider cultural influences and how these modify the life cycle. According to McGoldrick (2011), each stage of the family life cycle has tasks and challenges that must be negotiated in order for the family to successfully navigate successive stages. If challenges are not successfully met, subsequent stages may be compromised or the family may dissolve.

The single adult living independently of his/her parents is a stage added in the late twentieth century as an increasing number of middle class young adults postponed marriage in order to pursue higher education or to work. The primary task of this stage is to establish economic and emotional independence from parents. The challenge, particularly during economic downturns and high unemployment, is to become or remain economically independent from the parents. In Latino families, as will be discussed in Chapter 2, the independence of late adolescent and young adult children may not be as valued as it is in other ethnic groups. Thus, efforts to move out and become "independent" may be viewed as disloyal or a break from the relational connection to the family that is expected by the immigrant or less acculturated parents. In such families, this stage may be postponed until marriage, the time when it is culturally accepted among traditional Latinos for children to move out. My father used to say that women should leave home either in a white dress or in a coffin. I found an acceptable alternative for an immigrant family: I left home to pursue an education. It was still a time fraught with anxiety for my mother who became depressed as she found herself more socially isolated and experiencing a role shift and a drastic change in her cultural meaning system. Who was she if I was not there for her to mother?

Marriage: the Second Stage in the family life cycle is an expected event, especially among Latinos who hold traditional values. The primary task for the newly married couple is to establish boundaries around the new relationship as separate from the families of origin and to balance loyalties between the new family and the family to which they belong (family of origin). There are a number of challenges a newly married couple may encounter: meddlesome in-laws; cultural, religious, or ethnic differences that interfere with the formation of the new family; financial problems; and the possibility of moving away from the parents, which can constitute another migration for the couple or their respective families. Leaving home may trigger memories of earlier migrations and their attendant crises, challenges, or traumas, creating distress for all involved. There are a number of crises the newly married couple may encounter, including not having had permission to marry the partner, conflicts with family of origin, or marriage due to an unplanned pregnancy. According to family theorists, these circumstances may signal future trouble for the couple as they may render more difficult the negotiation of subsequent life cycle stages.

The ***birth of the first child*** is a significant developmental milestone for any couple. Among some Latinos, despite being married, a separate family unit may not be recognized until children are born. Couples without children of their own may not be viewed as separate or independent by their traditional parents. The principal task of this stage is to solidify the marriage before having children in order to withstand the challenge of including new family members and to balance pre-established roles to include parenting. Multiple challenges need to be negotiated: differences in ideas about parenting, negotiation of equitable distribution of workload, balancing the marital, parental, and worker roles. A number of crises may ensue: difficulty balancing multiple roles, difficulty including the child into the couple dyad, or including the partner when the focus is on parenting a small child. Differences in parenting ideals or practices between the family of origin and the new parents may result in the perception (or reality) that grandparents are meddlesome, particularly when grandparents convey the attitude that they know best or try to take over parental duties, which is more likely to happen in multigenerational households (Falicov 1998). Differences in the degree of *familismo* between partners may increase the tension if one partner desires a greater involvement of grandparents while the other prefers stronger boundaries between them and the in-laws. Clearly, the more children a couple has—or the closer the age of the offspring—the greater the number of adjustments and challenges the couple may face. In more traditional families, the involvement of extended family in childrearing and the help of older children in raising younger ones may reduce the stress faced by the couple that has to parent and to work for a living.

The next significant developmental milestone occurs when ***children begin school***. In many families, this stage begins much earlier when babies begin day care. For the parents, especially the mother, this is the beginning of separation from the child, which may occur when the infant is only a few weeks old. This can be a very challenging time for women who work. Significant stress may accompany efforts to balance the parenting and worker roles, to return to work (if either parent stayed home), and to continue to balance extended family and partner expectations. A long-term consequence of developmental crisis during this stage can be attachment problems and/or separation anxiety in either the child or the parent; in addition, couple conflicts may result from women feeling overburdened because household tasks are not shared to their satisfaction by their partners.

Adolescence is a challenging time for most parents. The primary tasks of this developmental stage include allowing increasing independence of the adolescent child while maintaining rules but increasing flexibility. Latino parents are described as authoritarian or authoritative (Flores 2005); at times, such parenting practices make it difficult to balance cultural expectations nuanced by the parents' own socialization with the demands of modernity. Additional challenges include negotiating differences between partners regarding appropriate levels of independence. Crises may occur when these differences cannot be bridged, resulting in marital discord, adolescent behavioral problems, or conflict between grandparents and parents. In some cases, the adolescent may become the identified patient if the couple is in crisis. The youth may "act out" in order to bring the parents together and rally around their child's "problem" and, thereby, prevent a separation (Bernal 1990).

In the ***Launching Stage***, the primary task of parents is to prepare the adolescent to leave home. As stated, in some Latino families, leaving home is not a cultural ideal. Thus, parents may not be prepared for letting their youth leave for college, move out on their own to seek work, or leave with roommates or intimate partners outside of marriage. Additional challenges may result with regard to disagreements between the parents as to how and when a child can and should leave home. After the last child is launched, the couple needs to find each other again and reestablish a relationship that may have been neglected due to the demands of parenting and balancing multiple roles. Among some Latinos, the importance accorded to children and childrearing is far greater than maintaining a close intimate relationship. Contemporary couples may maintain greater balance between themselves and their parenting roles and, thus, experience less "empty nest" than more traditional couples. For those whose primary role was childrearing, the anticipation of the empty nest may lead to symptoms of depression, reopen the wounds related to the losses of migration, or create dysfunctional patterns that keep the child from leaving. In turn, such family crises can result in the pseudo-independence of a child through teen pregnancy or behavioral or mental health problems (Falicov 1989; Bernal and Flores-Ortiz 1990).

Recently, the ***Boomerang Stage*** has been added to the life cycle theory to incorporate the return of adult children to the parents' home either alone or with their own nuclear families (Rasheed 2010). The challenges inherent in this stage have to do with renegotiating personal and collective space and rebalancing roles. In my own personal situation, my married daughter, her husband, and two daughters returned to live with me after living in another state for two years. Our household transformed in a short five years from that of a divorced woman living alone to an extended family of a young married couple living with their (now) three children and my daughter's stepson, and me. Included in the negotiations was allocation of space, relationship boundaries, shared expenses, and decision making regarding the children. Whether or not they should or could move in with me was never an issue. My son-in-law had concerns about my living alone post-divorce. He wanted to move in to support and protect me. In my view, my home was the family home to which my daughter and her family could return at any time. We support and care for each other because "that is how it is done."

The last stage of the family life cycle is referred to as the ***Empty Nest*** when the children have left home; the challenge now is for the couple is to renew the marriage or partnership without children, rebalance roles, and include grandchildren, if present. Among many Latinos, the empty nest never truly occurs; culturally, they are expected to continue the connection to their adult children by becoming involved with their grandchildren, or, in some instances, they are expected to continue to support adult children who, by reason of economics or psychosocial issues, cannot become fully independent (J. M. Cervantes 2004). This stage often coincides with middle age and the mid-life crisis of one or both partners; if the partners have not maintained their marital relationship, divorce or separation may occur. As previously stated, among traditional Latinos, this crisis is less likely to happen if the couple adhere to traditional cultural roles and their familial self is more dominant than their independent self.

Also included more recently, the ***Aging Family Members Stage*** addresses the challenges of providing for older parents while still raising children or supporting adult children. Latino families and other collectivist groups may experience less dissonance with the need to form multigenerational households to address the realities of the aging of grandparents and the need to become their caregivers (Flores 2008). The tasks and challenges of this stage entail dealing with the involvement of grandchildren and partners of adult children as well as facing the health crisis of old age while striving to maintain dignity and independence. My mother lived with my nuclear family after my father died. We took care of her until she decided to go to her country to die. There, her son took care of her; I traveled frequently to see her; and I supported them financially during the last ten years of her life. My children expect that they will have to do the same for their father and me despite my protestations that they do not have to do so. The cultural values of *familismo* have been passed down to the next generation more through modeling than as an explicitly stated expectation.

The life cycle model has been criticized because it reflects the realities of middle class, European American families to a greater degree than the context of working class and ethnic-minority groups. The model also assumes a linear progression and pathologizes those who do not follow the[20] stages sequentially (Rasheed 2010). In addition, the model is not sensitive to the particular challenges of immigrant families. Clearly, the life cycle is more complicated when divorce and remarriage occur along the way, creating a blended family. However, the model is helpful in understanding at what points families may face developmental challenges or crises that need attention in order to function to the benefit of all its members. Particular challenges may result from pregnancy before marriage as the couple may not have time to solidify the couple subsystem before a child arrives; therefore, they must negotiate two stages simultaneously. In cultures where childrearing is more important than the couple relationship, the couple may continually struggle with balancing parental and marital roles. In such cases, women may be dissatisfied with the marriage and become symptomatic, for example develop depression or anxiety (Flores-Ortiz 1993; Hirsch 2003).

The life cycle model points to particular times where crises may occur. Couples face a greater risk of separation or divorce during the second stage of marriage if they cannot balance family of origin obligations with the new family unit or during the stage of adolescence when normative changes overstress a couple without a strong foundation or during the Empty Nest period when the couple may see no reason to stay together once the children are grown (Carter 1998).

For Latino families, migration and the process of acculturation may also lead to crisis points as the families need to negotiate "cultural borderlands," the zones of similarity and differences between and within cultures (Falicov 1998). As stated earlier in this chapter, the need to negotiate or modify cultural meaning systems and cultural expectations, which can be disrupted by migration, may also complicate the family life cycle. Acculturation implies adoption of new behaviors, attitudes, and, sometimes, values, which can cause conflict within the family.

This chapter has provided an overview of the MECA model, highlighting the influence of migration and related legacies, social context, and the family life cycle on the formation of Chicano and Latino families. Chapter 2 offers a more detailed analysis of the influence of values, race, culture, gender, and class on the functioning of diverse Latino families.

ENDNOTES

1. The terms Latina and Latino are used throughout this book to refer to persons whose cultural and historical origins are from Mexico, Central, or South America. The terms Chicano and Chicana are used to denote children of Mexicans born or raised in the United States or persons who prefer that ethnic identifier. The term Hispanic is used when referring to writings where that term is utilized. It is important to note that the use of ethnic identifiers is politically charged for many Latinos and varies by geographical location, identification with the US and country of origin, and generational level in the US, among other factors.
2. This is an important fact given widespread policies in the US to ban bilingual education and other discriminatory practices that prohibit the use of languages other than English in the workplace. It may well be that the home is perceived as the only safe place where the ancestral language can be spoken.
3. See Salvador Minuchin, Braulio Montalvo, Bernard G. Gurney, Jr., Bernice L. Rosman, and Florence Schumer, *Families of the Slums: an exploration of their structure and treatment*, published in 1967 by Basic Books, N.Y.
4. The American Family Therapy Academy, the American Family Therapy Association, The International Family Therapy Association, and dozens of state family therapy associations, for example.

5. See for example, Oscar Lewis, *The Children of Sanchez*, and William Madsen's writings about Mexicans in South Texas.
6. Literally means co-mother. This is a form of fictive kin that develops when a woman becomes godmother or *madrina* to another's child. This cultural and/or religious pattern expands the family network from solely blood relations to non-consanguinial kin. The masculine pronouns are *compadre* and *padrino*.
7. A mixed status family is one in which one partner is an authorized US resident by virtue of birth or status, and one partner is an unauthorized immigrant. In such families, some children may be unauthorized while others may be citizens by birth or residents through status adjustment prior to age 18.
8. Cultural humility is a term coined by Melanie Tervalon and Jane Murray Garcia (1998) to describe an attitude and a set of practices rooted in the belief that cultural competence is unattainable. Instead, health professionals must engage in life-long learning and critical self-examination about the populations they serve. See Melanie Tervalon and Jane Murray-García, "Cultural Humility Versus Cultural Competence: A Critical Distinction in Defining Physician Training Outcomes in Multicultural Education," *Journal of Health Care for the Poor and Underserved,* Volume 9, Number 2, May 1998, pp. 117–125.
9. For example, terms of endearment used among Latinos reflect this racialized identity. The use of *huera,* meaning blonde or light skinned or *prieta*—darker skinned—are common among Mexicans and others who use their national equivalent to describe the skin color and racial features of family members. From an early age, children learn that skin color and phenotype matters. Quintana and Scull (2009) note that "Latino children develop ethnic identifications and identities under challenging circumstances" (82) partly because parents often "ethnically socialize their children in indirect ways" (81–82), for example, by the use of racial descriptors, such as *India* (meaning dark skinned like an indigenous person) or *huera.*
10. Immigrants are generally referred to as first generation; their offspring are considered second generation; and the grandchildren, third generation; and so forth. Many Mexican origin individuals in the southwest have roots prior to the Treaty of Guadalupe Hidalgo and may not identify as either Mexican or Latino but, rather, as New Mexican, for example, or as Spanish or of Spanish descent. The Chicano Movement of the 1960s (see Acuña, 2007, *Occupied America: A History of Chicanos*, 6th edition, New York: Longman) raised the consciousness of many US Mexican origin people and led to the adoption of the terms Chicano and Chicana to represent either Mexican origins or political identification with the struggle for justice of Mexicans in the US.
11. These are traditional Caribbean dishes of rice with pigeon peas, shredded beef, fried green plantains, or fried sweet ripe plantains. In other households, Mexican, Honduran, or Salvadorian dishes are prepared regularly, even by second and third generations.
12. Directed, written, and produced by Gregory Nava and Anna Thomas, and starring Jimmy Smits, Edward James Olmos, Esai Morales, Constance Marie, and Jennifer Lopez, *Mi Familia* (1995) offers a poignant view of the multigenerational legacies of migration and the complicated efforts to find a sense of belonging in an often hostile environment.
13. See for example, *Enrique's Journey* by Sonia Nazario (Random House 2006). Nazario documents the harrowing journey of a young boy left in Honduras by his mother as he travels through Central

America and Mexico atop train cars as he attempts to reach her, finding both the mother he longed for as a child and the promise of a better life for his own partner and child left behind.

14. See Ruth Behar's edited anthology, *Bridges to Cuba*, which chronicles with poems, stories, and essays, Cuban Americans' intellectual connection to their homeland.
15. I use the term "frozen" to refer to the ways in which families adhere to the dominant culture values that informed their development whether or not these are useful or applicable in the new social context. It is as if the family or individual took a snapshot of their life pre-migration and tried to recreate it in the new context. This may work for them as it provides cultural continuity. However, for their offspring, frozen cultural values may result in either adoption of stereotypic views of their culture, particularly since these may be reinforced in the media, or in rejection of aspects of their parents' culture that, in turn, can lead to intergenerational conflicts.
16. Core values, traditional and contemporary value orientations, and how these affect family life are discussed in more detail in Chapter 2.
17. Collectivistic cultures emphasize the needs and goals of the group as a whole over the needs and wishes of each individual. In such cultures, relationships with other members of the group and the interconnectedness between people play a central role in each person's identity. As a result, values of respect, interdependence, humility, saving face, and personalism are valued more than independence and individualism.
18. A more detailed analysis of family structure and organization will be provided in later chapters.
19. The *Quinceañera* or *Quince* is the celebration of a girl's 15th birthday, which historically signaled her entry into womanhood. Among wealthy Mexican families, it served as an introduction to society akin to the cotillion. In the nineteenth and early twentieth centuries, the *Quince* was also used to announce a young woman's availability for marriage. In the US, the *Quince* may have more of a religious or cultural meaning than with readiness for marriage. See Norma Cantu, *Chicana Life-Cycle Rituals in Chicana Traditions: Continuity and Change*, edited by Norma Cantu and Olga Najera-Ramirez, (2002), University of Illinois Press.
20. The applicability of the model to blended or step families and LGBTQ families has received some investigation (Janice Rasheed, Mikal Rashid, and James A. Marley [Rasheed 2010], Sage Publications, Beverly Hills, CA).

CHAPTER 2

THE INFLUENCE OF CULTURAL VALUES, RACE, AND CLASS ON FAMILY FUNCTIONING

INTRODUCTION

Mexican American and Latino families have been studied since the 1950s by sociologists, anthropologists, and psychologists (Peñaloza 1986). Early accounts of family life tended to rely primarily on cultural deficit models of analysis that were grounded on comparisons of these families to an idealized "European American norm." Literature from psychology tended to exclude a more nuanced analysis of the influence of structural integration or lack thereof (Falicov 1989 and 2013) on the ways in which families were organized and functioned. Sociological and anthropological studies also essentialized Latino culture, as if it were monolithic, thereby creating stereotypic accounts of Mexican American and Latino family life[1]. In general, family problems were seen to result from the culture of the family or their lack of assimilation to or adaptation of presumably more functional European American family patterns. It was not until the late 1960s and early 1970s that Chicano and Latino scholars began to study families through broader lenses (Keefe and Padilla 1987; Minuchin et al. 1967). These authors argued that Chicano and Latino cultural values were not the root cause of family problems; instead, it was the family's experiences with discrimination and inequality that resulted in family problems.

In the 1980s, with the emergence of family psychology and a shift towards a broader analysis of the family as a system that operates within and is influenced by a larger social context, more attention began to be paid to the role of socioeconomic class on family functioning. However, it was not until the mid-1980s and the work of McGoldrick, Giordano, and Garcia Preto (1982) and Falicov (1989), among others, that Latino families began to be studied holistically, paying attention to the influence of ethnicity, race, class, and gender on how families form and function. While foregrounding the position of Latinos within the larger US society, Falicov (1989), Bernal, and colleagues (1982, 1984, and 1986) also argue that understanding Latino values is crucial to the analysis of how Latinos construct the idea of family and give meaning to the experience of family life.

This chapter examines the role of cultural values in the formation and functioning of families at various points in the family life cycle. The ways in which the family's intersectionalities (ethnicity/race/class) also influence family organization and functioning is examined through case vignettes, as well. The importance of gender and the gendering of family members is considered, particularly as it relates to the negotiation of power and the performance of roles within the family.

ROLE OF CULTURAL VALUES IN LATINO FAMILY LIFE

The family became the central social unit of Latinos during the colonial period; Spaniards and other Europeans brought to the Americas a value system that privileged a patriarchal and patrilineal family organization. During this period, a caste system based on nativity, indigeneity, color, and gender also influenced family formation (Fuentes 1992). Spanish nobility held the highest social position with the indigenous holding the bottom of the social class (Johnson and Henderson 2003). To preserve racial purity and ensure control of the "landholdings" the Spanish Crown established laws that only recognized as legitimate children those who were born within the marriage of two Spaniards. The offspring of Spaniards and native women, whether born of rape or voluntary union, were not considered legal heirs. Thus, the importance of legal Catholic marriages to maintain the caste/class system.

Likewise, to ensure the power of the Crown, a set of values became reified, among them familism—the expectation of loyalty to the social group connected by blood and kinship ties—and respect to authority, elders, and people of a higher class. These values were instilled through education and religion. Identity was linked to a familial self and family name, which, in turn, situated the individual within a family group linked to a particular class. Men held the power and the privilege, and they were expected to form a family and produce heirs. They were not expected to be monogamous but to be discreet. Patriarchal privilege included the right to have as many women as they chose. *Machismo* emerged as a set of rules of conduct for men that included chivalry, honor, and responsibility towards the Crown, the Church, and blood kin. Virility was also valued, often resulting in the pattern of forming *casas grandes* and *casas chicas* (Paz in Johnson and Henderson 2003). The former, literally, the big house, was the family home where the wife and legitimate children lived. The latter referred to the home where a man's mistress and illegitimate children were housed. A "good man" provided for all his women and children and generally was admired for his landholdings and his progeny. Spanish women, on the other hand, were expected to be faithful as a way to ensure racial purity and preserve the family name. Religion was used to strengthen the expectation of sexual purity. Girls were expected to be like the Virgin Mary, pure, virginal, devoted, and pious. Their role was to protect the family name and support the husband, as well as raise children who would honor their father. A Virgin-Whore dichotomy was created that was also racialized. Becoming a legitimate wife, *la señora* was the highest aspiration a woman was expected to have (Flores 2013; Hurtado 2003). All other women a husband might have, *las otras,* the others, had no value; they were cast as whores who did not threaten the *señoras'* status because they were not the legal wives nor were they "ladies." The sexuality of "good women" was to be controlled by their fathers, brothers, and husbands. The others were cast as wanton, licentious, and immoral. Given their lack of morals, they could be used by men of higher status at will. Indigenous men, who had suffered the indignity and trauma of conquest and who carried legacies of oppression, were punished if they so much as looked at a white man's woman. According to psychoanalytic Mexican writers (Diaz-Guerrero 1956; Paz 1997), this historical context gave rise to the dark side of *machismo*—men who both loved and hated women, who blamed women for their own *mestizaje*, and who engaged in hypermasculine behaviors—fighting, womanizing, drinking—to mask their trauma, their grief, and their feelings of inferiority.

The colonization of indigenous people in the Americas left a legacy of cultural hybridity, intergenerational trauma, and the potential for troubled intimate relationships. Within the Spanish caste/class system, those born in Spain had highest value, followed by *criollos,* Spaniards born in the Americas. *Mestizos*, those of indigenous and Spanish descent, were generally illegitimate and marginalized, as were mulattos (Spanish-African descendants), Africans, and indigenous inhabitants of the colonies. Colorism, the value ascribed to people based on their skin color and phenotype, became important markers for social desirability or marginalization. The value of "respect" also became important; it was demanded of those in a lower social location and expected of children and spouses and extended family members. Social approval and social desirability were important to maintain one's social location and codes of interpersonal conduct—personalism—to ensure that protection of the family name was developed and taught. The concept of *el que dirán,* what will people say, became an important element of parenting. However, these Spanish values were also influenced by the indigenous value system of collaboration, mutuality, and interpersonal accountability. Personalism also entails regard for the well-being of others and indirectness in confrontation and communication in order to not offend, to "save face." The value system during the colonial period in the Americas was transmitted by education, religion, parenting, and *dichos*, sayings. For example, *hoy por ti y mañana por mi,* today I do for you, tomorrow you do for me, is reflective of the mutuality that informs personalism.

Prior to the conquest, the primary social group had been the clan; children were raised communally, and their identity was connected to the land and the ancestors (Flores 2013). Parents and community elders were expected to root the children into the values of the group and help identify the child's destiny (Tello 2008; Flores 2013). These values were maintained, to varying degrees, during the colonial period due to the marginalization of the indigenous and the *mestizo*; however, enculturation to "Spanish ways" was carried out through Christianization efforts. What emerged over time in the Americas was a hybrid culture that valued family connections, in part, because the family was often the only source of support, and yet it maintained some indigenous values, including collectivism and social accountability, as well.

In the study of families, values can be viewed as mirrors of the culture; they can be traditional, transitional, or contemporary. Values also can be viewed as idealized, ideal, and enacted. Idealized values refer to the cultural scripts of how things "should be;" ideal values refer to the conduct and behaviors the family and/or individuals aspire to or prefer; and enacted values are what people actually perform.

Among Latinos, idealized values include virginity before marriage and fidelity thereafter for women, but not necessarily for men. Other idealized values are respect for elders, solidarity (*compañerismo*), cooperation, and collectivism.

With increasing acculturation and modernization, individuals' behaviors mirror idealized values less and less. Moreover, in modern times, Latino families continue to reflect hybrid cultural influences. Familism, personalism, and respect are cultural ideals. Respect for elders, those in authority and extended kin, are central to Latino parenting (Flores 2005); interpersonal accountability, social desirability, and protection of the family name are still highly valued. The degree of adherence to these cultural ideals varies, depending on the family's and individual's level of acculturation to non-Latino cultures, exposure to other cultural values, and parenting practices.

Adherence to traditional values also may be influenced by the family's relationship to the means of production. At any given time, values and social class interact to influence specific family behaviors, attitudes, or practices (see Table 1, Bernal and Alvarez). Values can be viewed as mirrors of the culture: they can be traditional, transitional, or contemporary. In addition, values can be viewed as idealized, ideal, and enacted.

Idealized values refer to the cultural scripts of how things "should be" (Falicov 1998 and 2013; Flores 2013); for example, the enculturation of female children to be modest, loyal, and pure in order to marry well. Ideal values refer to conduct and behaviors the family and/or individuals aspire to or prefer; for example, "a well educated child" is one who is obedient to parents and other family members, is respectful, humble, and deferential. An ideal man is one who is honest, hard working, responsible, chivalrous, and loyal (Flores 2013). Enacted values are what people actually perform.

Ramirez (1967 and 1969) among others posit that values often are at the core of people's behaviors and less likely to change *initially* due to contact with other cultures.

Table 1. Social Class and Cultural Values in Family Life

		TRADITIONAL	TRANSITIONAL	CONTEMPORARY
Urban families	Wealthy			
	Middle Class			
	Working Class			
Rural families	Large Land Owners			
	Small Farmers			
	Migrant Farmers			

Adapted from: "Cultural Perspectives in Family Therapy," Cultural Perspectives in Family Therapy, pp. 38.

Attitudes and behaviors may change more rapidly to facilitate adaptation, particularly among immigrant adolescents and children. With increasing acculturation and modernization, individuals' behaviors may mirror idealized values less and less, often resulting in conflict between parents and children.

The Lopez Family

Jose and Elena Lopez were referred to therapy after Elena slapped Judy, their 15-year-old daughter, and the school became concerned when Judy told her teacher about it. It was not the first time Elena and her daughter had engaged in a loud altercation. According to Elena, since age 13 Judy had become *malcriada e irrespetuosa* (bad mannered and disrespectful). Elena described her eldest child as a loving, kind, *considerate* girl until then; overnight it seemed she had become willful and disrespectful. Judy stated that her mother was rigid, authoritarian, uptight, and disrespectful. The conflict that led to the referral began when Elena told Judy to change clothes. According to Elena, her daughter was dressing inappropriately—her shorts were too short and her shirt showed too much cleavage. When Judy refused to change, Elena "lost it" and told her daughter she looked like a slut—*pareces una puta.* In response, Judy called her mother a bitch and, horrified, Elena slapped her.

Jose indicated that he did not know what to do. It seemed to him that his wife had overreacted, but he agreed that Judy had become a stranger to him as well. His sweet little girl had become an angry, disrespectful teen. Their two younger children, an 11-year-old boy and a five-year-old girl, were terrified by the hostile climate in the home.

Jose was a second-generation Chicano; Elena had immigrated to the US as an adolescent. Both held strong familistic values; however, Jose appeared to be more flexible in his parenting style. He believed that Judy should have more independence than did his wife. His wife was raised by traditional parents and stated that she had difficulty adjusting to the US when she first arrived. Her parents lived as if they had never left rural Michoacán; they were strict, and Elena did not date until she started working after graduating high school. Elena did not challenge her parents' ways and was comfortable growing up in a primarily immigrant, Mexican community. Jose had met Elena at the grocery story where she worked and he often shopped when he visited his parents in "the barrio." Traditional parents raised him, but as a male, he had been granted a lot of freedom. He went to college and became an architect. He had paid off his parents' home when he obtained his first job and had later bought himself a home in an ethnically diverse suburb. When he asked Elena out, she told him he would have to come ask permission of her parents. He thought that was "cute" and agreed. When he told his mother, she was happy that he was interested in someone *de buena familia.* His mother equated traditionalism with being a good family—that is, one that raises proper well-mannered and modest daughters.

Jose went to visit Elena's parents accompanied by his mother to ask permission to date Elena. The two families soon became friends, and within one year, Jose and Elena had married both legally and in the church as was the Mexican tradition. Elena was 20 and Jose 25 years old when they married. Elena worked until Judy was born and then remained home raising the children. She was a loving and devoted mother and wife. They tried to raise their children with traditional values of familism and respect. They visited each other's parents on Sunday after church, and although they had a diverse group of friends, Elena felt more comfortable with other Mexican women and felt a bit out of place with the more educated couples in Jose's social network. The couple spoke Spanish at home, as Elena did not fully master English in school, and she was more comfortable speaking Spanish. Jose was more fluent in English than Spanish, so he often "slipped" into speaking English with the children. Judy was bilingual but preferred to speak English. This was a bone of contention between her and her mother. Elena felt hurt that her daughter spoke less and less Spanish and often answered her in English. Elena felt disrespected.

As Judy entered adolescence, both parents felt ill equipped to parent a girl who was influenced by US culture more than their own Mexican ways. Elena was particularly concerned about her daughter's sexuality and tried to control it as her parents had controlled and protected her own. However, Judy was not as docile as Elena had been. Judy was offended that her mother had called her a slut when she was a "good girl." The family had reached an impasse.

The "problem" in this family can be understood as reflective of cultural differences. Elena espoused traditional cultural values, largely idealized, and had difficulty supporting Judy's biculturality. She relied on cultural scripts learned in the home—the dichotomization of good vs. bad females—and feared that her daughter would be judged as "bad" due to her style of dress. Judy, whose primary exposure to Latino and Mexican culture was through the media and immediate family, was presented with objectified sexualized images of Latinas. She did not feel she was dressing inappropriately; rather, she was dressing like all her other Latina friends. She did not see her disagreement with her mother as disrespectful; instead, she was attempting to express her views and exercise her own agency. Jose felt torn; he wanted to support his wife's parenting views but felt she was too strict. He loved Judy and admired her "spunk" but could not let her disrespect his wife.

What often leads to this type of problem is lack of communication about underlying values. Parents often do not realize that cultural values have to be taught; they are not assimilated by osmosis. Moreover, US-born-and/or-raised children are exposed to multiple cultural influences. They also must negotiate more complex identities than did their immigrant parents. In family therapy, Jose and Elena were invited to discuss their underlying value systems and expectations, as well as the concerns they had regarding Judy's place in the world as a female and as a Mexican origin woman. In turn, Judy was able to ask questions of her parents and negotiate age-appropriate activities. They all worked on improving communication. The parents were largely unaware of the sociocultural demands and the degree of marginalization their daughter faced on daily basis. Judy did not know her parents as people informed by the cultural values of their families of origin. Conversations about these issues and foregrounding the family's history and current social context helped the parents and Judy negotiate the normative challenges of adolescence. The mother-daughter relationship took some time to heal; but, eventually, both came to understand and respect their uniqueness and similarities.

At various points in the family life cycle, different levels of adherence to traditional values may create conflict. For newly formed couples, balancing the social, individual, and family self, as well as loyalty expectations from the family of origin may create stress. Traditional Latino families tend to be child centered; that is, parenting may take a more prominent role than the couple relationship. If Latinas and Latinos with different levels of adherence to this value co-parent, one may feel neglected if the mother focuses more on being a mother than being a wife. If women try to balance both roles, more traditional family members may criticize her as selfish or chastise her for not being sufficiently self-sacrificing.

A devoted mother who focused primarily on parenting raised me. My father, who lost his mother at a young age, supported my mother's focus on being a mother but found sexual partners outside the marriage. As a function of acculturation and education, as well as migrating to the US in my youth, my values became transitional. I balanced parenting with education, work, and marriage. As is the case with many Latinas, trying to fulfill multiple roles and obligations was a challenge and often fraught with stress. I was able to fulfill my academic desires and career aspirations because my mother helped me parent my children. Both of my parents filled in whenever I was too busy (Flores 1998). My daughter demonstrates a more contemporary value system—she is a caring mother and wife who works and takes time for herself. She juggles her multiple obligations and roles with greater ease than I ever did. She is reflective of more contemporary values—familistic with a strong familial and individual self. Moreover, as did my mother before me, I support my daughter and her husband's parenting of three small children. In this way, I also fulfill my own cultural script of being a good grandmother.

SOCIAL CLASS

Historically, family organization and the enactment of gender roles was influenced, if not determined, by the family's relationship with the means of production. Agricultural families included small and large landowners, peasants, itinerant workers, and migrant workers. In rural settings, these are still the predominant class; these families tended to be larger, extended, with more children, and dependent on the seasonal nature of agriculture. For example, families who experienced the *tiempo muerto,* the time of year when there is no cultivation of crops, could also face the migration of males and young adults who follow other crops (Bernal and Alvarez 1983). In these families, gender roles may be more flexible. While the male head of household may hold most of the decision-making power while he is at home, once he leaves, the woman emerges as head of household and exercises greater authority. Some women refer to this as "borrowed power" (Flores and Valdez Curiel 2009). When the man returns, she needs to cede the power. In such families, male and female children may be exposed to shared power and less strict division of labor along gender lines.

The Industrial Revolution brought about mass migrations and a shift from agricultural economies to wage labor; in turn, families became less extended with fewer children and often with more rigid gender roles. Likewise, the Industrial Revolution gave rise to a class structure that was not necessarily land based but, rather, based on the accumulation of wealth. The upper class enjoyed wealth, while the middle class strove to attain it, and the working class worked to survive; their production increased the wealth of the upper classes (Bernal and Alvarez 1983). The upper class enjoyed leisure time and the privilege of its social position. Gender roles tended to be more fluid while still showing traditional practices and expectations. Many of the roles and tasks typically ascribed to women—taking care of children, cooking, cleaning, and so forth—were performed by maids, who were women from the lower classes, thereby, freeing up the time of wealthy women to pursue education or leisure activities. The middle class typically consisted of women and men who worked and raised families with the aid of extended family members or older children who helped with parenting and domestic chores. The poor remained poor and strove to survive economically and to raise children often in adverse conditions that limited education and upward mobility.

In most of Latin America, the class divisions that were created during the colonial period remain. Industrialization and neoliberal policies have created greater economic disparities, resulting in domestic and international migrations both unauthorized and authorized as people pursue greater economic opportunities. Likewise, political instability and repression in many Latin American countries, as a result of military dictatorships, civil wars, and US intervention, also have destabilized economies and contributed to migration to the United States (Falicov 2013).

In the later twentieth century, economic shifts in the United States gave rise to the working poor and, as a result of the welfare system, a non-working class. Many Latino families fall into the category of the working poor. Their values often reflect the importance of hard work and education as a way out of poverty, yet their social position and limited structural integration (Rumbault 1994) prevent many of their children to attain the American dream of upward mobility. Farm work remains a large source of employment for immigrant Mexicans; blue-collar jobs in construction and manufacturing are also prevalent among Latinos as are service jobs—housekeeping, maintenance, and landscaping/gardening. Few Latinos hold managerial or professional jobs. Therefore, the majority of Latinos occupy the lower middle class or are working poor (US Census 2010).

Likewise, increased poverty and "economic downturns" have resulted in homeless families and family systems that "break down," resulting in dysfunction (i.e., individual and family social and mental health problems). Latino children in foster care have increased significantly in the past decade (Casey Family 2010); this is indicative of a substantial breakdown in the family's ability to parent and protect its children, a core cultural value (Flores 2013).

Families may share more similarities with others of the same class level from different ethnic or racial groups than with families of the same ethnicity of higher or lower class. Irrespective of the class position Latino families occupy, core cultural values influence patterns of interaction and determine what is considered important. The enactment of core values, however, will be influenced by the intersection of class and culture (Bernal and Alvarez 1983; Falicov 1989). At any given time, families can be "plotted" in terms of class and culture, thus, producing great within-group diversity. As stated earlier, according to Williams (1990), with increasing upward mobility, the gender and family roles of Chicana/os change significantly. Women, for example, may define themselves more in terms of their professional than their family role. Stress related to internal conflict regarding cultural loyalty and adherence to traditional values may accompany such shifts in identification and variation in the performance of gender roles (Flores-Ortiz 1993).

All these factors are influenced by generational and acculturation level. More recent immigrants, particularly from rural areas of Mexico and Central America, may hold more traditional values. Their children, born or raised in the US, may evidence transitional values. The second generation and beyond, as well as those who have attained higher education and social status, may hold more contemporary values, which primarily nuance gender relations, power dynamics within the family, and sexuality (Flores 1993; Flores and Valdez Curiel 2009). In the Lopez family, as discussed earlier, the husband's education and career opportunities positioned them within the middle class. The family took vacations, owned a home, and appeared to enjoy the benefits of their social class. Yet in the home, Elena tried to create traditional family life; she stayed home and raised children. She helped them with homework, prepared all the meals, and, while her husband "helped," she was still the one who was primarily responsible for the household management. They parented their children together; however, Elena held more traditional views of parenting. She was authoritative; she believed children should not question their parents' dictums and should display respect. Elena expected Judy to be modest, collaborative, and kind. When Judy entered adolescence and began to express her own views and imitate her peer's style of dress, Elena became authoritarian. Conflict arose between them. In this family, the class position influenced some of their behaviors; however, the mother's value system remained traditional while Judy's showed transitional values as did her father's. Elena's worries about her daughter's behavioral changes were nuanced by her anxieties about Judy's nascent sexuality. Elena "heard tapes in [her] head" of her mother's admonitions about a girl's proper conduct—how she should act, dress, talk—to gain and maintain respect from men. Elena worried that her daughter's appearance and style, which to her was provocative and inappropriate, would draw the attention of men with bad intentions, who would perceive her daughter as wanton and cheap. Elena was unconsciously influenced by the *puta thing* (Souza 2001), the fear of *el que dirán,* and that her daughter would be criticized and harmed by a misperception of who she was. When Judy called her a bitch, Elena was so offended she responded with aggression, something she had never done before and regretted immediately.

As the parents externalized their internal value system, their three children began to understand their parents' position on many issues and comprehend how cultural values and their parents' own upbringing influenced their expectations of how their offspring should behave. Judy came to see her mother as a woman who held traditional Mexican values that often clashed with United Statian adolescent views of what was appropriate behavior and dress. Judy's ethnic identity was not fully solidified (Hurtado and Gurin 2004). Her peer group was a mix of both Latina and European American friends; she preferred to speak English, and while she spoke Spanish with her maternal grandparents, she did not identify as Mexican but as Latina; however, she did not have a clear sense of what that meant. She stated that she was not white and did not feel fully accepted by white peers. Thus, she socialized mostly with other second generation Latinas, some of whom were Mexican origin. Until the family therapy sessions, she had not given much thought to what it meant to identify as Latina or how her parents' culture and upbringing had affected her own.

PARENTING

Latino parenting practices are described as largely authoritative (Flores 2005); the children are rooted into the value system of the parents by example and by explicit and implicit expectations. Often through sayings or *dichos,* parental messages are conveyed regarding the way to remain on the good path and become a productive citizen. Tello (2008) argues that in pre-Colombian times, parenting was the responsibility of the community and the family. Children were to be rooted into their clan and actively taught the values of the people through example and stories. Through colonization and more recent times, parenting has increasingly become the responsibility of the nuclear family, which often must root the child to the family's culture while the schools acculturate to the dominant culture.

The Lopez family, as described above, raised their children with largely traditional values that were reflected in how they lived, their high degree of contact with their families of origin, their church participation, and the expectation that family loyalty and respect were fundamental. Although they lived in the suburbs, they visited with grandparents who had remained in ethnic enclaves or *barrios.* Jose had tried to move his parents closer to their home, but his father and mother preferred to stay *entre Mexicanos.* Jose's father had experienced a great deal of racism and discrimination when he first came to the US as a *bracero.* He did not want to again experience that marginalization by moving into a more affluent, predominantly white neighborhood. He liked walking to the *mercado* and chatting with older immigrant men. His wife also preferred to remain in her *barrio* where she knew the people and had lady friends on whom she could rely for social support.

Jose and Elena modeled respect for their parents, concern for their well-being, and loyalty. At the same time, they modeled traditional gender roles within the home. Jose was not waited on by the women to the same degree as his father, but he also benefitted from the male privilege traditional Mexican values afford men. He was the provider; therefore, he did not have to help out at home. Judy and her younger sister were already noticing that their brother had fewer chores than they did. Judy felt it was unfair that she should have most of the chores simply because she was a girl and older. Elena became upset when Judy challenged these home practices, which she considered sexist. Elena viewed her daughter's disagreement as disrespect; Judy saw her complaints as legitimate.

Authoritarian parenting practices are characterized by rigid rules typically along gender lines and with little room for negotiation. Children are to be seen and not heard. In these families, patriarchal practices are more stringent. Sometimes men eat first, children second, and women, last; women wait on the men and boys hand and foot from mothers to wives to daughters. In traditional and transitional families, boys tend to have less responsibility with home chores; often, they are expected to help their fathers with more masculine chores—washing cars, yard work, etc.—reflecting the view that the home is women's turf and the outside world is the realm of men (Flores 2005).

More acculturated and higher-status families may practice more contemporary values and exercise less traditional gender role assignments. Their parenting practices may be seen as more egalitarian or democratic (Flores 2005). Boys and girls are taught basic family values, and their gender role expectations may be more age dependent than based on cultural ideals of how men and women *should* act or behave. Among my working class origin college students, traditional masculine values of being responsible, respectful, and loyal remain deeply ingrained despite US nativity and higher education. The women often hold more contemporary values regarding gender roles while simultaneously holding highly familistic views. Often, the women experience internal conflict if their behavioral patterns do not match the underlying value system inculcated by the parents (Flores 2013).

In general, immigrant parents find it more challenging to parent US-born-or-raised children since these children are exposed to the cultures of the school and the peer system; over time, these cultural influences may appear to take over the values taught or expected at home. Some parents feel that they are losing control of or influence over their children; therefore, they may become more authoritarian in order to feel that they are doing a good enough job of preparing their children to follow the good path. Others seek ways to support their children's biculturality while others feel overwhelmed and become permissive; they perceive permissiveness to be less stressful than trying to maintain traditional values in a social context that does not appear to support their efforts. In general, Latino parenting practices vary by class, nativity, level of education, and acculturation. However, the fundamental values of respect, familism, and personalism remain, to varying degrees, across generations of Latinos.

COUPLING

Cultural values and social class also influence how couples form and negotiate their intimate relationships. Patriarchal notions of power and privilege influence heterosexual couple relationships among Latinos. The stereotypical description of a traditional Latino couple is that of a submissive, docile wife and an overbearing, controlling *macho*. While such relationships do exist, the partnering of Latino males and females is far more complex and largely influenced by class, education, the value system of the partners, and the larger social context in which they live and love.

Latino adults tend to marry and stay married. In 2012, there were 11.6 million Latino households. Of these, 62.3% were married couple households. Over 60% of Latino married couples had children under 18 living in the home; 65.7% of Latino children lived with both parents. Only about 28,000 children lived with only their father and about 131,000 lived only with their grandparents (US Census: *America's Families and Living Arrangements* 2012). Latinos have had lower divorce rates than other ethnic groups and tend to marry other Latinos with greater prevalence than they marry European Americans or other ethnic or racial groups.

Latino families generally expect their children to marry and form their own families. In Latin America, women tend to marry young unless they pursue an education. Typically, by age 23, it is expected that women will be married. A common expression about women over 23 who are unmarried is *las dejó el tren*, that is, the train left without them. The fear of many parents is that the older the woman, the less likely she will be to marry. The underlying concern is that a woman *needs* the protection of a man who will support her financially and emotionally. Without such a man, she will then be left *para vestir santos,* to dress the saints in church. The preference has been that women partner with older males who will have had time to obtain an education or stable employment and, therefore, will be ready to settle down and provide for their family. Marriage, both legal and by the church, is expected among the economically privileged and more religious families. A common pattern among those with lower education or social status is to form unions outside of marriage. Among the more acculturated and educated Latinos, living together is seen as an alternative or precursor to marriage while higher education is pursued. Traditional parents will often "look the other way" and pretend that their daughters are not participating in premarital sex or unions, reflecting underlying cultural values and concerns about appearance, *el que dirán,* and protecting the family's reputation.

Family theory suggests that the more support a couple receives from their families of origin, the easier the transition to married life will be. The more disapproval or conflict the union generates among extended family members, the more difficult it will be for the partners to negotiate the transition to married life. Cultural value differences may present particular challenges. The Lopez found support for their union. Both Elena and Jose had immigrant parents who held traditional views. Jose's mother was relieved that her son was marrying "a good girl." Elena's parents were pleased that she was going to marry an educated man, a son of Mexicans, whom they assumed held similar familistic values. Although Jose was more acculturated than Elena, they shared highly familistic views. They had more diverse views of parenting, but Jose enjoyed Elena's traditional attitudes towards home life. She did not expect him to do much work around the house. When he "helped," she was appreciative. However, she believed that running the home was her duty, which she performed with great pride and love. Jose stated that he enjoyed that privilege although he would have been perfectly happy with helping more. Elena did not want him in the kitchen. She considered that woman's work. Judy was beginning to resent that she was expected to become equally skilled in household tasks for which she had no passion. She grudgingly did chores, not to learn how to do them to her mother's standards, but to prevent conflict with her mother. She argued that she did not see any point to learning to iron or do laundry well as she planned to become educated and "send her clothes out." Elena heard those statements as a devaluing of her beliefs. She felt she was failing at raising a daughter who would make someone a good wife.

Until very recent times, Latino cultures pathologized homosexual and lesbian unions. Although laws and policies have changed in the past few years, popular views remain mixed. Most families hold heteronormative ideals and struggle with accepting children who are queer. Many parents prefer the "don't ask, don't tell" approach to their children's sexuality. Forming couple relationships within this larger sociocultural context adds multiple layers of complexity (Espin 2013).

Mariluz and Eva

Mariluz, a South American immigrant, fled her country during a dark period of political repression. She had been a college student at the time and had to seek political asylum in the US after her brother was kidnaped and murdered by the military. In the US, she became an attorney and human rights activist. She married and had two children. However, she "always knew" she was attracted to women but tried to repress her feelings given her refugee status and the multiple traumas she had endured. She stated that she could not imagine having to deal with any more persecution. At a political rally, she met Eva. Mariluz was 35; Eva was 28. A child of Mexican immigrants and a politically active, queer, feminist Chicana, Eva was Mariluz's role model of a well-integrated identity. They became friends. Eva had grown up in a large extended family that held very traditional values. Mariluz was estranged from her Italian-American husband but considered herself "very married."

Initially, Eva was unaware that Mariluz was falling in love with her. Eva stated that she had never wanted to become involved with anyone who was ambivalent about her sexuality. From early childhood, Eva knew she was lesbian. She came out to her parents in adolescence; they initially rejected her largely due to their conservative religious views. Eva struggled to complete high school as an emancipated minor and earned a scholarship to attend college. She became an activist in college and "came out to the world." At college, she found a supportive community of Chicanas who were feminist and accepting of queer sisters. She worked for a community-based organization that advocated for women and immigrants' rights. Her life was full, she stated, and did not need the drama that a relationship with Mariluz might bring.

The two women formed a strong friendship based on their shared political views and activism. Eva became enamored of Mariluz's children, who were 11 and 13 when they met. They began to spend more and more time together as family. One day, Dolores, Mariluz's 13-year-old daughter, asked Eva if she was going to be her mother's new partner. Eva was confused by the question. Dolores looked her "straight in the eye" and told her it was obvious the two were in love. Eva was shocked—and relieved—that the truth had been said out loud. Eva and Mariluz realized that they were in love and wanted to be together. Full of fear and trepidation, they spoke to Danilo, Mariluz's 11-year-old son, and tried to make sense of the changes about to happen in their lives. Both children were supportive. Eva, who had never wanted to own property, bought a flat and had Mariluz and the children move in with her. Mariluz was living in a home bought by her husband. When Mariluz told her husband that she was filing for divorce, he promised to fight her for custody to protect his children from "her deviancy."

Mariluz's mother wept when her daughter told her she was moving in with Eva and that they were going to be a family. However, her mother already had lost her only son to a military dictatorship and was not willing to lose her daughter, as well. Consequently, she asked her daughter for time to get used to this new reality. Eventually, she became Mariluz and Eva's most ardent supporter, testifying in court on their behalf during the protracted custody battle that ensued. Having been rejected by her family once before, Eva did not reach out to her parents when Mariluz's estranged husband began to threaten and harass her. However, when Eva's three brothers found out that a man was threatening their sister, they came to her defense and support. One of Eva's brothers was a police officer in another county; he asked his colleagues to pay this man a visit. The harassment ceased. Eva's mother could not acknowledge that her daughter was in an intimate relationship with another woman but welcomed Dolores and Danilo into her family. Over time, the children "won her over," and she began to call them her grandchildren.

The early stages of couple formation were challenging for Mariluz and Eva due to the pervasive homophobia they encountered in the legal system. Despite being an attorney, Mariluz had difficulty finding a compassionate attorney who was willing to represent her. Her estranged husband was part of a well-established and affluent family with political contacts. They were willing to spend whatever amount of money was necessary to remove the children from Mariluz's custody. The treatment of Mariluz by her former in-laws became increasingly hostile with open racist attacks against her former status as a political refugee and as a Latina. They labeled her as an ungrateful woman who had used their son to get residency (which was untrue) and had had "anchor children" to remain in the US. Their vitriolic attacks were inflamed by the anti-immigrant fervor of the early twenty-first century. In addition, they argued that two lesbians would pervert their grandchildren. Moreover, while they had tolerated Mariluz's *latinidad* (how she embodied and enacted being Latina), as she was light skinned and highly educated, they were incensed that Mariluz was leaving their son for "a low-class, dark-skinned Mexican."

Eva and Mariluz spent thousands of dollars in legal fees and for "experts" who could testify in court, evaluate the children, do family studies, and so forth. The children had to enter therapy to deal with the conflict, and the mothers began couples therapy to deal with the stress on their relationship. Mariluz was granted a divorce, but the custody agreement was not reached for two more years. The father obtained 50% custody and often violated the visitation agreements, dragged Mariluz to court on multiple occasions, and falsely accused them of child abuse until Dolores refused to visit him any more. Dolores confided that her father raged against Mariluz and Eva and frequently threatened to take the children to Italy and never return. Danilo was particularly affected by his father's rage. He decided to go live with his father when he was 13 in the hope that this would appease him. It did not. Danilo then went to live with his paternal grandparents for two years and eventually returned to Mariluz and Eva. He remained in therapy for years to deal with the trauma caused by his father's anger and his grandparents' racism.

In couples therapy, Mariluz expressed her feelings of guilt—she was plagued by "shoulds": she should have suppressed her feelings and her love for Eva for the sake of the children; she should have anticipated her ex-husband's rancor and the response of her former in-laws to the situation; she should have sacrificed her desires for the sake of the children. She found it ironic that she had fled a military regime to fall prey to an intimate terrorist who tried to destroy her, compromised their children's mental health, and damaged her relationship with Eva. Eva, on the other hand, was unwavering in her support for Mariluz and reiterated that although she had anticipated the drama, the sorrow was worth it. She had found her soul mate and no threats from any man or his well-heeled family would break their bond. Her motto in life, Eva stated, was to push forward against all odds, *contra viento y marea,* doing what was necessary to protect her family and her marriage.

Seven years after the divorce, Mariluz's former husband who was then in his mid-40s married a 20-year-old woman and started a new family. He stopped harassing Mariluz and stopped seeing their children. Dolores and Danilo, then, respectively, a young adult and a late adolescent, had to return to therapy to deal with their father's abandonment and to make sense of why he had done such damage to them. In 2012, Eva and Mariluz celebrated 20 years together; they married legally in early 2014 and now live peacefully, without drama, and continue their fight for social justice.

Mariluz and Eva were able to withstand the assaults to their relationship and their own integrity because they had shared values of family, loyalty, commitment, and a profound love and respect for each other. Perhaps if they had not had such passion for social justice, they might not have been able to remain together in the face of such attacks. Despite their differences in nativity and social class, particularly in their families of origin, they were able to create *familia* and transcend the challenges they faced.

GENDER ROLES: POWER AND SEXUALITY

In the context of a patriarchal culture, traditional gender values and roles emerged, which mirrored each other as *complementary.* The man *should* be the *head* of the family and the woman the *heart*; the value of a man is based on how well his family is run (how disciplined are the children and how supportive is his wife). Within this complementarity, if each observes the respective role, he will be respected (if not feared) and she will be revered. This complementary also is nuanced by *machismo* and *Marianismo*. *Machismo* is the code of conduct of a man and a direct legacy of Spanish conquest and its sequelae (Paz 2003); it entails men being physically strong, potentially virile, indomitable in character, and stoic. The better man is the man who can drink the most, defend himself the best, dominate his wife (even using physical force if necessary), command the respect of the children, have more sexual relationships, and engender more sons (Falicov 1998). This cultural archetype may be attenuated by socioeconomic changes, education, and/or migration.

At the core of the archetype, is the expectation that a man should please women and behave like a gentleman. An important part of being a good *macho* is being devoted to the women in his biological family, his mother above all others. Mexican movie stars of the

1950s, most notably Pedro Infante, embody this cultural ideal. Contemporary Chicano and Latino men may hold some aspects of the ideal consciously or unconsciously yet strive for more egalitarian relationships with women.

The counterpart of machismo, *Marianismo*, refers to the docile, self-sacrificing ideal of good womanhood. The term literally means "cult and emulation of the Virgin Mary." A traditional socialization script calls for loyalty to family, especially men, overvaluing of sons, protection of spouses, and absolute respect for and obedience to parental authority. While education and migration may reduce adherence to a strict practice of this role, it may be a core value, which surfaces at various points in the life cycle. In addition to *Marianismo, hembrismo* refers to the qualities of strength, endurance, courage, perseverance, and bravery embodied by some women. The strength of Latinas in the face of adversity is admired as long as the moral codes imposed upon them are not violated. *Hembrismo* may operate in the work sphere while *Marianismo* is practiced at home. Clearly, the balancing of cultural expectations in the face of cultural change can be very stressful for both men and women.

Power, defined as the ability to exercise agency and make decisions affecting the self and other(s), is determined, partly, by the degree of adherence to traditional values. In traditional couples, men decide over the family as a whole, but women exert authority over the domestic sphere. Women can exercise their power as long as it does not *directly* challenge or sabotage male authority. Women often use the indirect power of subtlety and persuasion; thus, it may appear to outsiders that they lack power in the relationship when, in fact, they may hold significant power. In egalitarian relationships, it is presumed that couples *discuss, hear each other's opinions, and jointly decide.*

In summary, in traditional Latino families, gender roles tend to be shaped by class and patriarchal notions of who should do what. Women's identities are nuanced by the value of familism and the expectation that a woman is the heart of the home and family. Women often are socialized with the image of the Virgin Mary as the guide for their behavior. Purity, docility, sacrifice, and service to others represent "the good woman." Deviation from those traits may be viewed as selfish. Men are to be the protectors and providers for the family. More modern ideas and attitudes about shared responsibility in the management of the home and the raising of children are associated with higher social status and greater educational access. In most of Latin America, however, traditional values regarding gender continue to influence how men and women live their lives.

Power is often negotiated between partners on the basis of home/work responsibilities and income earned. In more modern couples, important decisions are made jointly and power is shared. Conflict can arise in couples when each holds a different view and value regarding gender roles and decision-making power (Flores 2005; Flores-Ortiz, Andrade Palos, and Valdez Curiel 2002). Elena and Jose were able to co-parent and create a fairly harmonious family because they had similar familistic views; although Jose was more egalitarian in his gender role views, he was willing to enjoy the privilege accorded by his wife's more traditional gender role views. He was not oppressive, and she enjoyed taking care of her family by being at home and assuming most of the home duties, which she had begun to teach her daughters, but not her son. In this way, she was perpetuating a more traditional role assignment to her children based on gender.

Julian and Emma

Julian and Emma met in college; she was a second generation Chicana who considered herself feminist. Noelia, a single mother and an immigrant from El Salvador, raised Julian. As the eldest child of a single parent, Julian learned from an early age that he had to help out. He learned to cook by age eight, he did laundry by age 11, and was fairly good at house cleaning since he joined his mother on the weekends when she cleaned other people's homes. However, his mother often would tell him that he should marry a traditional woman who would take care of him. He did not give much thought to his mother's "advice" until he and Emma moved in together in their last year of college. Suddenly, Julian realized that he was expecting Emma to cook, clean, and take care of him. Emma was shocked since Julian had seemed quite independent and capable of doing these things for himself. When Noelia came to visit, Emma noticed that she seemed to disapprove of their life style. Noelia commented that the apartment could be cleaner and told Emma how Julian liked his shirts ironed. Emma was furious. She and Julian began to argue and considered separating.

Julian realized that although he had been actively involved in domestic duties since early childhood, he had done so out of necessity, not because these chores "belonged" to him. When he did housework, he was helping his mother or Emma. He believed these activities were, indeed, women's work. Emma expected and encouraged "an attitude adjustment" to preserve their relationship.

Emmanuel and Leila

Not all men raised by single women learn domestic duties or have more egalitarian ideas about gender and gender roles. Emmanuel was the eldest of four; his father left the family when he was 10. Thereafter, the family faced significant economic adversity. His mother worked two jobs. His sister Lucy took over the household duties and Emmanuel was elevated to "man of the house." He was not expected to do housework but to help with the discipline of the younger children. In adolescence, Emmanuel began to come home late and act "like a man." His mother gave him a great deal of latitude, as she was raised traditionally, and she was passing on those practices to her children both out of necessity as well as tradition. When Emmanuel met Leila, a third generation Chicana, he liked her independence as she also worked and went to school at the local junior college. However, when she became pregnant, their relationship problems began. Emmanuel had lacked an appropriate role model of responsible masculinity. He did not know how to be a father or a partner. Leila insisted he "step up" or else. He went to work to support them but insisted that she do all of the housework, which she found to be unfair since she had to nurse an infant and tend to her baby's needs. They lived together for a few months; however, each then returned to live with their respective parents because Emmanuel was not ready to be a husband/father and was in danger of repeating his father's pattern of abandonment. He seemed unable—and unwilling—to negotiate their conflicts. They had been unprepared to assume the parenting role. Although he remained minimally involved with his son's upbringing and paid child support, his relationship with Leila ended. He subsequently partnered with a more traditional woman who "made no demands" on him.

SEXUALITY

The American Psychological Association (2010) defines sexuality as encompassing a person's sex, gender identity and expression, and sexual orientation. Thus, in most families, boys and girls are socialized according to their gender and taught family and culturally expected ways to express their gender identity. Most cultures and families rely on heteronormative assumptions about "proper behavior" and privilege a heterosexual orientation. In traditional Latino families, the expectation is that girls will remain virgins until marriage while boys should gain sexual experience prior to settling down (Hurtado 2003). The general assumption has been that men have greater sexual desires and needs than women. Women who are more sexual are likely to be labeled as wanton, licentious, and promiscuous. Those with more transitional and contemporary value orientations are less likely to hold the double standard regarding sexuality. Nevertheless, most Chicana scholars of sexuality find that even highly educated Latinas and Chicanas often hold conflicting and stressful views regarding their sexuality and the right to enjoy their sexual lives (Castañeda 2013; Flores 2013 b; Flores 2013c; Hurtado 2003).

Sousa (2002) posits that the gender socialization of Latinas supports the dichotomization of women into good and bad objects. With the implicit and explicit threat of being labeled *puta,* Latina girls are encouraged to disconnect from their bodies, suppress and repress their sexuality, and problematize their desires: concerns with sexuality begin in childhood and continue throughout their life cycle (Flores 2013). Sexual identity is an integral part of healthy identity formation (Hurtado and Gurin 2004; Zavella 2003). However, the sexuality of young Latinas is problematized and associated with their reproductive patterns. Worries about teen pregnancy tend to be a concern of both parents and social scientists, who view Latinas' high fertility rates (when compared to European American women) as problematic regardless of whether or not the young women find it so. Latino boys tend to engage in sexual behavior earlier than girls; however, there is less concern in the family and among social scientists about this pattern except for worries about sexually transmitted infections and overall health (Aguirre Molina and Betancourt 2010).

According to Chicana lesbian writers (Anzaldua 1987; Perez 1991 and 1993; Trujillo 2003; among others) it is the perception that queer Latinas are less constrained by traditional gender sexuality that makes them so dangerous to patriarchy. However, Espin (2013) and Hurtado (2003) find that regardless of their sexual orientation, Latinas continue to struggle with gender socialization and patriarchal cultural expectations about women's proper behavior and expressions of their sexuality.

BEGINNING TO THEORIZE ONE'S FAMILY

In order to fully understand Latino families, it is critical to analyze them in context (see Figure 1 in Chapter 1) and to view them as a system of people connected by blood, history, experience, love, marriage, friendship, etc. In addition, consideration must be given to the historical events that have shaped each family over time. Multigenerational patterns and legacies become visible through the use of genealogy (McGoldrick, Gerson and Petri 2008). A vertical and horizontal analysis of each family helps understand the present—the family's social location (socioeconomic status, educational levels of its members, employment patterns and status)—by considering its past.

HOMEWORK ASSIGNMENT

1. Reflecting on your family in the present, determine their social location (SES, educational level, employment status)
2. Reflecting on your family history:
    a. What do you know?
    b. How long has your family been in the US?
    c. Who came first to the United States (or who came first to them)?
    d. What is the racial/ethnic composition of the family?
    e. Where are the silences?
    f. What are the secrets?
3. Reflecting on the values held by your family:
    a. Which values are more traditional?
    b. Which values appear to be in transition?
    c. Which values could be considered contemporary?
4. How are gender roles assigned and negotiated in your family?
    a. What are the gender roles evident in your family?
    b. Who does what?
    c. Who decides what?
5. To what extent are your gender values reflective of your family's cultural ideals?
    a. How have gender roles changed or evolved over the years?
    b. What accounts for the changes in gender roles?
    c. In what ways has your family's history of migration impacted or changed gender roles?
    d. Who holds the power?
    e. How is power negotiated between partners?

ENDNOTES

1. See, for example, Oscar Lewis, 1961, *The Children of Sanchez: the Autobiography of a Mexican Family*, NY: Vintage Books, and William Madsen's studies of alcohol abuse among Mexican Americans, "The Alcoholic Agringado," *American Anthropologist*, 1964, vol. 66 (2), 355–361.

CHAPTER 3

FAMILY FUNCTIONING THROUGH CULTURAL LENSES

INTRODUCTION

Families can be viewed as systems evolving over time as their members pass through and negotiate the various life cycle stages and developmental milestones. As stated earlier, Latino families must be viewed contextually. McGoldrick and Hardy (2008) propose that families are embedded within a geopolitical structure; the policies that derive from that structure influence how well the family functions within society. Likewise, family functioning is determined, in part, by the family's value system and by the ethnicity, race, and class of its members, which positions it within a particular ecological niche (Falicov 1989). The gender and sexual orientation of family members also influence its functioning. The family and its members' religion or spiritual practices also will nuance how family members relate to one another and to the outside world.

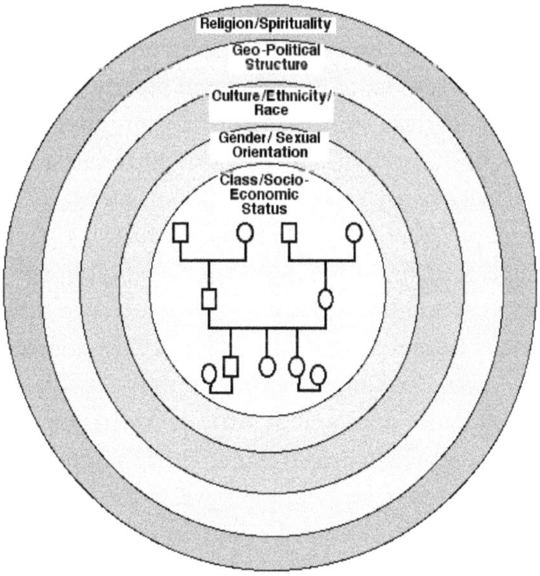

Figure 2: Genogram in Multiple Contexts

Monica McGoldrick, "Genogram 1.3: The Genogram in Multiple Contexts," Context and Connections: Transforming Life Narratives: Workshop Presentation in Venice, Italy. Copyright © 2008 by Monica McGoldrick. Reprinted with permission.

This chapter examines family functioning among Latinos

while describing three major family theories that have been useful in the evaluation and treatment of Latino clients. First, a brief overview of family systems theory is presented; followed by a more detailed description of contextual intergeneration, relational justice, and narrative approaches; and third, the use of genealogy to appreciate family uniqueness and identify patterns of resilience and dysfunction is reviewed in some detail. The overarching questions inherent in this chapter are: *What constitutes well-being in Latino families? What factors contribute to fairness and justice and unfairness and injustice in Latino family relations?*

FAMILY SYSTEMS THEORY

Murray Bowen suggested that individuals couldn't be understood in isolation from one another but, rather, as a part of their family. He posited that families are systems of interconnected and interdependent individuals, none of whom can be understood in isolation from the system. Furthermore, Bowen viewed the family as an emotional unit. That is, the emotional state of one member reverberated throughout the system and affected the other family members (Bowen 1978).

Bowen also introduced a number of important concepts that were further developed by other theorists. He highlighted the importance of **differentiation of the self** from parents and other family members; otherwise, **Emotional Fusion** might occur, resulting in adult psychopathology. Clearly, differentiation is a western concept inherent in individualistic cultures. Families from collectivist cultures might not emphasize individuation; instead, they may promote emotional interdependence (Bernal and Flores-Ortiz 1990). Bowen also introduced the notion of **family triangles**; that is, alliances or coalitions between two family members to the exclusion of a third. For example, a mother and son might form a tight coalition to the exclusion of the father. Such a coalition might become dysfunctional over time, fostering emotional fusion between mother and son as well as a lack of differentiation of the son from his mother. In his early writings, Minuchin (1976) argued that not all triangles are problematic. For example, among socioeconomically disadvantaged families, Puerto Ricans, and other Latinos, as well as African Americans, intergenerational households and intergenerational triangles (grandmother-mother-grandchild) could be functional and, in fact, necessary for family survival.

Bowen considered the nuclear family, that is, the family created by the partnering or marriage of two adults, to be most important in the shaping of children. He also recognized the contributions of the extended family both as a resource and as a source of intergenerational dysfunction, particularly if individuals were not sufficiently differentiated. He noted that couple conflict and the symptoms in a spouse or child all could be understood as emerging from the family emotional system while being influenced by the **multigenerational transmission processes**. This is the process whereby the relational anxieties and problems of previous generations are passed down to subsequent ones, especially if there was insufficient differentiation. This concept was an important contribution that underscored the importance of considering and studying the family's history to comprehend (and treat) the problems that nuclear families might develop.

Bowen argued that the triangles and anxieties of previous generations were passed down to subsequent ones and, thus, could contribute to the development of family problems. Bowen also coined the term "**Family Projection Process**" to describe how children develop symptoms when they get caught up in the previous generation's anxiety about relationships. For example, a child may develop a school phobia when the parents' marital conflicts escalate as a result of one family's disapproval of the marriage and their efforts to sabotage the union; the parents must then "work together" to help their child and shift the focus away from their marital distress. The parents "projected" their anxiety about possible separation onto the child who, in turn, "is afraid" to leave the parents and go to school. In effect, within systems theory, children are considered to be the emotional barometers of the family. Well-adjusted children are indicative of a family system that is functioning well. Children who manifest emotional problems may be mirroring distress that is most likely in the parental subsystem; however, that could be the result of intergenerational conflicts or lack of differentiation of one partner from his or her family of origin.

Bowen also introduced the concept of **Emotional Cutoffs**, the efforts by family members to try to escape emotional fusion in a family (Bowen 1978). Cutoffs can be attained by physical and emotional separation or distance and are distinct from efforts at separating from the family in young adulthood in order to attain greater independence. Bowen also noted the importance of **Sibling Positions** within a family. Likewise, the emotional climate and context of the family at the time of the child's birth might influence his or her position and role within the family. A replacement child, after the death of a loved one, for example, might be at risk for developing separation problems, emotional fusion, and adult mental health problems.

In traditional Latino families, the firstborn male tends to hold a very privileged position; he is often a co-parent with the mother if the father is absent or disengaged. The younger siblings are to respect him and seek his approval and advice. If all family members share that value, sibling relationships may be smooth. If the parent overburdens the son, he may rebel. If he is parentified, that is, if he is expected to fill the emotional needs of his mother, which he may be ill equipped to do, he may become symptomatic or pseudo individuate. In that case, he may act as if he were an adult (by engaging in drinking and stereotypic male behaviors) while remaining economically and emotionally dependent on the mother. A cultural pattern could, then, become problematic and contribute to mental health problems in the son, the mother, or the siblings.

Bowen's early theories influenced the development of family psychology (Guerin 1976). Other important concepts in family theory address the structure of the family (nuclear, extended, blended) and the subsystems within the larger system (see Carter and McGoldrick 2010; Guerin 1996; Minuchin 1974). The executive subsystem would include the parents as architects of the family and decision makers. The sibling subsystem would consist of the children. Family boundaries, the degree to which family members understand their place, their roles, and expectations of them held by other family members, are also important. Well-defined but permeable boundaries with clear lines of communication are considered optimal. Families with excessive closeness and diffuse boundaries are considered enmeshed. In these families, rules and roles may be unclear and "emotional fusion" is more likely to happen.

Because interdependence and reciprocity are cultural values among Latinos, emotional closeness is expected. Families may appear enmeshed to those who hold more individualistic values. This may particularly be the case in multigenerational households, where grandparents and parents collaboratively raise children, older children perform some executive functions, and smaller children may appear to have a closer emotional bond with a sibling or grandparent than a parent who is away at work most of the time. On the other hand, disengaged families are those where the boundaries are so strict that there may be reduced emotional closeness and minimal communication and exchange between subsystems. In such families, there may be an expectation that children leave home at age 18 and become financially and emotionally independent from the parents. This may be a cultural ideal in some families but may appear dysfunctional to other, more collectivist groups. Clearly, boundaries are important and contribute to family functioning if there is communication with clear expectations and roles. However, cultural values and class position, as well as family history and intergenerational patterns will also influence the structure and functioning of the family.

From a family systems perspective, a well-functioning family is one with a clear hierarchy—the parents constitute the executive subsystem—that clearly communicates between them and with the children. Every family member is aware of the rules and norms of the family. The parents facilitate the children's transition through their developmental stages while mindful of their own life cycle both as individuals and as members of a family. Boundaries are permeable so that children have access to the parents, and there is emotional closeness without fusion or enmeshment.

Latino families who hold traditional values may appear less differentiated and more enmeshed than middle class European American families. Communication patterns may be less direct and clear; in many families, triangulated conversations are more common. That is, to maintain balance and harmony direct confrontations are avoided and indirect messages are more common. For example, a mother may tell a child that a particular behavior displeased the father. The child is then expected to correct the behavior for the sake of family harmony. Within a monocultural context, this pattern may work, but, as will be seen in later chapters, within a multicultural context, an adolescent may opt for ignoring the advice since it did not come directly from the father; this can be viewed as disrespect by both parents (as seen in Jose and Elena's difficulties with Judy).

From a family system's perspective, a well-functioning Latino family is one with clear and permeable boundaries, emotional closeness within and across generations of the family, and where the values of respect, personalism, collaboration, and solidarity are enacted (Falicov 2013). Nativity, generational level, religious affiliation, class, and level of acculturation will determine the extent to which these values are adhered to or expected from the parents and grandparents.

A contemporary of Bowen, Ivan Boszormenyi-Nagy, who was also a psychiatrist, developed a family therapy theory that has been used extensively to understand and treat Latino families with a variety of problems, including substance abuse and intrafamily violence (see Bernal, Flores, and Rodriguez-Draguin 1986; Bernal et al 1999; Bernal and Flores-Ortiz 1990; Flores-Ortiz and Bernal 1990; Flores-Ortiz 1991).

CONTEXTUAL INTERGENERATIONAL FAMILY THERAPY THEORY

This model highlights the importance of studying families in context and across generations. The model consists of four dimensions of analysis: Historical Realities or Facts; Individual Psychology; Systemic Issues; and Relational Justice.

Historical Realities or Facts

This dimension deals with the facts, history, and legacies of an individual that are generally unchangeable; for example, sex at birth, gender, ability, birth order, race, and ethnicity. In the case of Latinos, important attention must be paid, as well, to the family's history of migration and the transgenerational legacies such migrations create. In addition, the circumstances surrounding birth and early development of family members may also contribute to particular patterns of functioning. A premature baby, for example, may become an overprotected child, especially if she or he is the firstborn and there is a family history of infant mortality and a privileging of firstborn males.

Individual Psychology

Unlike other family theories that focus exclusively on the nuclear family and family interactions, this model also privileges the individual psychology of family members. It is critically import to ascertain the meaning an individual gives to his/her historical facts and legacies. What does it mean to be a second-generation Chicano born into a working class family of Mexican immigrants who have struggled unsuccessfully to attain the American dream? How does that historical reality affect his self-esteem, ego strength, coping style, etc.? How does he see the legacies of his parents' migration affecting him, if at all? Likewise, what are the identity issues (race, ethnicity, sexuality, politics, etc.) each family member must negotiate and how do such issues affect the family as a system? How do the life cycle stages and degrees of dependence/interdependence of family members influence or affect the family as a whole? What are the challenges and opportunities each family member faces as a result of his or her nativity, generational status, gender, sexual orientation, class position, and so forth?

Systemic Issues

In addition to individual psychology issues, this model also examines both family of origin and nuclear family arrangements. Specifically, the type of family structure that is created, the degree of functioning, life cycle stages of the families of origin, and procreation must all be examined. In particular, a systemic analysis views the family life cycle as key to understanding the problems that develop at particular points in time (Carter and McGoldrick 2010). For example, immigrant Latino parents may experience anxiety and other psychological distress when their first child wants to leave for college. This is a normative part of the Launching Stage (see Chapter 1) and although desired by many parents, for immigrant parents, separation from a child may reopen the wounds created by migration-related losses. The fear of separating from the child may result in depression or anxiety in a parent and adversely impact the emotional well-being of the entire family.

Likewise, the family roles, rules, and norms must be understood within an ecological context of class, race, nativity, and overall social position. As Minuchin and associates noted in the 1970s (Minuchin et al. 1976), families often organize on the basis of need, forming triads across generations to raise children and support one another. Such arrangements, which do not mirror the middle class organization of an executive and sibling subsystem separate from the family of origin, are not inherently dysfunctional. Instead, if the women collaborate and the rules and roles are clear, then multigenerational households and arrangements can be functional.

As stated earlier, some family theories posit that clear and distinct but permeable boundaries are optimal for family functioning. Boszormenyi-Nagy argued that equally important is the degree of cohesion, closeness, and interdependence of a family *if* it reflects their cultural values system. Families should not be compared to a social science European American ideal of functioning without consideration of their ethnicity, race, and class. Furthermore, determination of the cutoffs, enmeshment, or disengagement of a family also must be culturally informed (Bernal et al. 1986; McGoldrick and Hardy 2005). As stated earlier, some Latino families may appear enmeshed because of the high degree of extended and nuclear family interaction and interdependence that is valued and performed.

Relational Justice

Boszormenyi-Nagy believed that *trust*, *loyalty*, and *mutual support* or *reciprocity* are the key elements that underlie family relationships and hold families together. Symptoms develop when a lack of caring and liability result in a breakdown of trust in relationships (Nichols and Schwartz, 1998). Boszormenyi-Nagy referred to these elements as relational justice. Ethical, fair, and just family relationships form healthy children and adults who are loyal and trustworthy.

Family relationships occur within a context of give-and-take. Central to relational ethics is the concept of balance. Balance, reciprocity, and an oscillating balance between give-and-take characterize ethical relations. Giving to others vertically (parent to child, adult to parent) earns credits or merits. Those who receive become indebted and must give vertically to balance the relational ledger over generations (children grow to become providers of their parents and so forth). Adults cannot collect from children or peers that which they did not receive from their parents. An oscillating balance also exists between giving and receiving vertically (between parents and children, grandparents and parents, extended family members and younger generations) and horizontally, among peers and siblings. If there is reciprocity in the giving and receiving, individuals maintain balance between merits earned by giving and the debits resulting from receiving. These merits and debits are earned both vertically and horizontally. Injustice occurs when there is exploitation or lack of reciprocity in family relationships.

Boszoremni-Nagy introduced other important concepts, including the degree of *entitlement* and the inherent right to fair treatment that are held by family members, which could be constructive or destructive. A loving, caring environment fosters a sense of entitlement that is balanced. Parents owe their children care, love, and nurturing. Early bonding and fair parenting practices lead children to develop **constructive entitlement**.

Exploitation, deprivation, or maltreatment fosters **destructive entitlement**, the ethical position that the world owes one what the parents did not or could not provide, resulting in *"a chip-on-the-shoulder attitude."* A child who is not cared for by his or her caregivers will grow into adulthood seeking such caring from partners who cannot fill the void left by parental neglect. Such early wounds also may result in self-destructive behavioral patterns (to be discussed in later chapters). Destructively entitled people attempt to collect from others what they did not receive and what they cannot give. Destructive entitlement is often at the root of couple problems and abusive parenting.

Furthermore, within families, relationships are rooted in **visible and invisible loyalties**. Families have rules about giving and receiving, which shape loyalties vertically and horizontally. Visible loyalties are those that are explicit and congruent. Visible loyalties foster balance and are grounded in reciprocity because trust and reciprocity constitute the fabric of connection among individuals. When relationships are fair and balanced, loyalty considerations are visible. Loyalty is expected visibly within families, particularly those rooted in collectivist values. Children are taught directly and by example the importance of loyalty to the parents, grandparents, and siblings, as well as extended family members. This loyalty comes from trust and fairness in relationships. On the other hand, invisible loyalties develop out of injustice.

Invisible loyalties are characterized by covert expectations and incongruent messages. They result from exploitation, imbalance, and lack of reciprocity. Invisible loyalties may be at the root of individual and family dysfunction. A child who is maltreated will experience soul-wounding and develop deep emotional scars. His or her love for the parent who was not trustworthy or accountable will be entangled with feelings of rejection, abandonment, and pain. He or she may feel a compulsion to exonerate the poor parenting received by being a less than accountable and trustworthy individual in both vertical and horizontal relationships. In this way, the adult who was a maltreated child or who experienced any form of relational injustice becomes invisibly loyal to his or her progenitors and is likely to replicate those patterns in subsequent intimate relationships. Can I be a better parent than my own parent was? Through individual and family dysfunction, we exonerate our progenitors and fulfill legacies of earlier generations (Bernal and Flores-Ortiz 1990).

Contextual intergenerational family therapy has been used successfully with Latinos whose emotional wounds manifest as addiction, depression, and family violence (Bernal, Flores-Ortiz, and Rodriguez-Dragin 1986; Bernal and Flores-Ortiz 1990; Flores-Ortiz 1993, 1996, 1999 a, b, c). This model has been particularly effective because of its consideration of the multiple dimensions of family life, including the family's historical realities or facts. Such an analysis is critical to understanding Latino families of varying generations and levels of acculturation.

In the mid- to late-twentieth century, two mental health professionals from Australia and New Zealand, David Epston and Michael White, began to offer workshops on a different form of treatment of individuals and families in distress (Beels 2009). They "decentered" the role of the master therapist and, instead, focused on collaboration with clients and organizations. Their ideas, which have developed and expanded globally, gave birth to what others have labeled narrative therapy. What was unique to the West about this approach is that it suggested that therapy itself could be oppressive if practiced from the perspective that a "master," a trained and certified "expert," had the solutions to others' problems. Both psychoanalysis and family therapy had converted "problems" into pathologies and people with problems into patients who *were* pathological. Family therapists often spoke of "dysfunctional families," suggesting that the family was sick, much as psychoanalysis had viewed the person as sick. White and Epston argued that the problem was not in the person; thus, the person was not the problem. The problem *was* the problem. Moreover, their approach resonated with many Latinos because of its emphasis on understanding the stories and narratives that influence and shape people's lives. Both White and Epston worked with marginalized and disenfranchised communities, including Aborigines, Maoris, and Samoans, as well as White Australians and New Zealanders, not as experts but as consultants who had to be accountable to these communities because of their class, race, gender, and sexual privilege (Beels 2009; Waldegrave, Waik, and Camb 2009). They stated that a "critique and deconstruction of institutional power in our public, private, and voluntary services is encouraged in a manner that honors diversity and enables sensitive therapy, other forms of service delivery, and policy making that genuinely reflect the range of cultural, gender, and socioeconomic experiences of citizens" (Waldegrave, Waik, and Camb, 2009, 85).

NARRATIVE- AND JUSTICE-BASED APPROACHES

The context of social and therapeutic problems is critical to their resolution, and [that] many of them stem from historical and structural injustice. ... contextual issues of cultural, gender, and socioeconomic equity as providing important insights into authentic notions of social inclusion and well-being, and encourages therapists, service

> *providers, researchers, and policy makers to take responsibility to ensure that these injustices are addressed, and become part of the public discourse about the sources and solutions of endemic social problems (Waldegrave, Waik, and Camb 2009, 85).*

JUST THERAPY

Developed by staff at the Dulwich Family Centre in New Zealand, Just Therapy is grounded on the belief that human problems are related to situations of injustice, particularly the marginalization of groups on the basis of race, gender, ethnicity, sexual orientation, ability, etc. Furthermore, histories of colonization, miscegenation, oppression, sexism, and racism foster multigenerational legacies of pain and disenfranchisement. These legacies influence how people understand or "story" their lives; narratives of empowerment and disempowerment can underlie people's problems. People in marginalized communities may "internalize" "isms" and create stories about themselves and their people, which may reduce agency, efficacy, and foster psychological "homelessness" (Hardy and Laszloffy 2005). As will be discussed later, these grand narratives can influence the way people live their lives. Healing entails re-storying one's life to increase agency, ability, and self worth. Such healing can happen optimally within family and community. Waldegrave and colleagues (2009) argue that we need to listen to each other's stories and help each other create more positive narratives to counter the dominant discourse that engenders or supports any form of oppression.

NARRATIVE THERAPY

At the core of Narrative Therapy is that people's lives are multistoried. No single story of life can be free of ambiguity or contradiction. No self-narrative can handle all the contingencies of life. The role of therapy is to bring these alternate stories out of the shadows and to elevate them so that they play a far more central role in the shaping of people's lives (M. White 1994).

Among the basic concepts of Narrative Therapy is that of the *saturated story*—that which other methods of treatment labeled "the presenting problem." The therapist facilitates the deconstruction of the saturated story by posing questions, which *externalize* the problem. For example, Latino couples often present with stories embedded within multiple stories. These stories often reflect the stories and narratives of others who are important to their lives (i.e, extended family members, in-laws, neighbors) or historical issues of justice/injustice. The central idea is that the couple (or the individual or family) does not own the story; instead, the story owns them—it has taken charge of their lives. The narrative therapist poses questions to help externalize the problem in order to deconstruct it and reconstruct it. It is important to be aware of cultural/familial embedded stories that oppress (for example, *el que dirán*—the concern with what others will think—which is a common worry among more traditional Latinos). Elena, for example, worried about what others might think about Judy, which in turn would be a reflection on her "bad parenting." Elena did not own the story of being a good parent. A grand narrative about proper sexuality and women's conduct, a legacy of the colonial period, owned her perception of her parenting. A therapeutic shift would be *como lo diré o como lo diríamos* (how would I or we say it)? In this way, the individual, couple or family owns the story.

In working with couples, the therapist might ask *how the problem is shaping or affecting the couples' life.* Through questioning, the consideration for alternative stories is generated, and the couple begins to develop an alternative story so that unique outcomes can be possible. For example, a therapist might ask, "*Señor, cuando dejó usted de ser esposo para convertirse en problema?*" (Sir, when did you stop being a husband to become a problem?) (Flores and Rivera-Lopez 2014). What couples and families often bring to therapy is the "gift" or the saturated story, which often reflects cultural grand narratives or the legacies/grand narratives of the parents; for example, migration stories, family stories, stories of political oppression/trauma/torture, or stories of biculturality and lack of belonging—*no ser* "*ni de aquí ni de allá*"—to feel that one is neither from "here or there."

In working with Latino families who are Spanish speaking, an important question is whether stories written in one language can be re-storied in another. We often ask of clients, "*Cuando usted llora en que idioma llora, en Ingles o en Español?*" With couples, if the nature of his problem is in one language and hers in another, how can they re-story a mutually satisfying and respectful narrative?

For Latinos whose grand narratives are of abandonment, the therapist needs to consider the following questions: How are we as children impacted by parental loss or abandonment through death, separation, divorce, or dysfunction in the parent? What is the dominant story for an individual who has suffered such loss? How can such narratives be re-storied?

When adults are not accountable due to their own saturated stories, dysfunction, illness, or responses to structural forces (for example, migrations to improve the family circumstances) children *may* grow up with a diminished sense of value. The dominant story may be: "*I am not important enough to be loved, for my parent to stay, to be taken care of, etc.*" This dominant story may lead to feelings of disentitlement or destructive entitlement as articulated by Boszormenyi-Nagy and Spark (1984).

Likewise, physical and sexual victimization in childhood creates a negative script for adult, intimate relationships. The sequelae are fear, disconnection from body, mind, or spirit. Post-traumatic stress disorder is the equivalent of *espanto* or soul loss in the indigenous emic system (Flores 2013). Healing from such victimization entails reconnecting mind/body/spirit, holding perpetrators accountable, and forgiving oneself (see Flores-Ortiz 1998, 1999 c).

Re-storying cultural narratives about alcohol and other drugs requires an understanding of the historical legacies of colonization and the use of alcohol by the conquerors to subdue the indigenous. There are roles in the culture: *el tecato, el vato loco, el hijo de la chingada, el pobre, y el pelado,* which evoke images of a castrated male who has no agency, a buffoon who covers his feelings of insecurity and self-hatred with grandiose masculinity and masks his pain with alcohol (Paz 1997). *El hijo de la chingada* refers to the *mestizo*, the "half-breed" product of Spanish conquest and colonization. *El pobre y el pelado* refers to members of the social underclass who may be poor but have dignity.

There is a link between dominant stories and alcohol and drug abuse that must be explored to understand the nature of addiction in Latino families (to be discussed in subsequent chapters). Likewise, the cultural views about alcohol need to be deconstructed—alcohol is central to having fun, the ability to hold one's liquor is a sign of masculinity (or of being a strong woman). How can these cultural notions be deconstructed and reconstructed to transform those roles and stories into more positive ones? The Family Centre proposes that healing from substance misuse is like a journey from one identity to another: from victim to survivor to well-balanced whole person (Smith and Winslade 1997). Healing is facilitated by promoting authentic connections and reconnections with the ancestral culture and worldview.

Narrative and Just Therapy approaches propose relational paradigm shifts and the co-construction of justice-based "preferred relational stories." With regard to historical and intergenerational trauma as well as relational injustice, the collaborative team (client, family, community, therapist) works on transforming "victimhood" to survivorship, and mindful of the external political context, the team co-creates a preferred story.

Transforming stories entails reconnecting to ancestral spirits and cultural stories before conquest and colonization; honoring the ancestors through constructive legacies; using humor and connection; and building healthy relationships and families through activism, balance and health (Waldegrave et al. 2003). My work with Latino students and clients over the years has utilized Just and Narrative Therapy approaches to promote health and the re-scripting of dominant stories that limited agency and perpetuated pain.

GENEALOGY AS METHOD

McGoldrick and Gerson (1985) developed a systematic method of obtaining one's family history in order to identify behavioral patterns, repetitive histories of family problems (early death, divorce, migration), and the ways in which context (Figure 3.1) may have influenced the family development over time. The authors encourage the use of geneaology in family therapy. As a first step, one should identify relatives on both sides of the family up to three to four generations or more, if possible. It is helpful to obtain basic information, dates of birth, deaths, marriages, illnesses, and to identify ethnic, racial and/or religious affiliations. Symbols are used as shorthand to determine the type of bond among family members; for example, married couples are connected with solid lines, unions (without marriage) with broken lines. In getting the family story, one can interview family members, particularly one who may be the family historian or genealogist[1].

When you interview your relatives, try to ascertain stories of migration or roles in that process (i.e., who was the bridge, mourner, etc.), even if you think migration is not relevant to your family. Listen for stories of cutoffs, disconnections from relatives, culture, language, etc.; ask about patterns of marriage, divorce, informal adoptions, etc. Inquire about roles, patterns of communication, rules about family life, and values and traditions, as well as illnesses, particularly chronic illnesses with a genetic component. Look for traumatic events, being mindful of "silences" around stories that may signal a reluctance to divulge information that may be too sensitive or a secret for someone else.

Once the information is obtained, the "family tree" can be drawn, using the symbols developed by McGoldrick and Gerson (1985) to denote conflict, over-involvement, or disengagement in family relations. Once the tree is complete, one can begin to identify patterns. From these patterns, one can theorize about the genesis of particular family problems, sources of injustice, or saturated stories that have affected the family over time. Likewise, family resources, sources of connection, and resilience can be identified.

WHAT IS A HEALTHY, FUNCTIONAL LATINO FAMILY?

Returning to the fundamental premise of family theory, a functional family is one that loves, nurtures, protects, and provides for its members. Among Latinos, those fundamental mandates of family life are nuanced by historical legacies and histories that can both promote resilience and survival and potentiate problems if the social context does not support the family's culture and race. To determine how well a Latino family is functioning a through evaluation of its structure, patterns of communication, historical realities, and ecological niche is necessary. Furthermore, each family is unique and must be evaluated in terms of how it is fulfilling its commitment to its members, not compared against a European American, middle class family ideal that may no longer exist, even for European Americans.

In our work, my colleagues and I find it helpful to assess the family's history of migration, unresolved issues related to that cultural change, degree of biculturality of its members, psychological rootedness, justice and injustice in family relations, and the dominant stories that may need to be transformed to create greater harmony and balance in family relations (see Bernal, Flores-Ortiz, and Rodriguez-Dragin 1986; Flores-Ortiz and Bernal 1993; Flores-Ortiz 1993; Flores-Ortiz 1999; Flores 2005). Each family that seeks treatment should be compared against itself and its ideals and realities. In collaboration, challenging problems and grand narratives can be deconstructed and reconstructed to promote greater healing. In the next few chapters, the most pressing problems faced by diverse groups of Latinos will be discussed.

ENDNOTES

1. A useful resource is Monica McGoldrick, 1997, *You Can Go Home Again: Reconnecting with Your Family*, NY: W. W. Norton & Company, or the newer edition, *The Genogram Journey: Reconnecting with Your Family*, published in 2011.

PART TWO

CHAPTER 4

WHEN LOVE IS NOT ENOUGH: INJUSTICE IN THE FAMILY

A well-functioning family is a system in balance that can negotiate transitions and resolve conflicts with fairness and consideration of the individual and collective needs of its members. Families are likely to face challenges at various points in the life cycle; family systems with good communication, shared values and goals, and permeable boundaries can successfully meet these challenges. A migration and separation from loved ones at any point in the life cycle can create significant challenges for families. As noted in earlier chapters, forming a new couple unit may be difficult if either partner feels overly loyal to his or her family of origin, has not attained enough emotional independence from that family, or if he or she faces larger social, economic, or cultural pressures than he or she is equipped to handle, for example, homophobia, racism, classism, sexism, poverty. The arrival of the first child can also challenge a couple, particularly if the partners have different expectations and ideas about parenting or if the in-laws desire more involvement than does either member of the couple. Likewise, balancing work/life can prove difficult for couples with varying degrees of adherence to cultural values and gender norms. In this chapter, I will explore some of the normative challenges families may face as well as the more serious problems contemporary Latinos experience. These problems are situated within the frameworks offered by McGoldrick (see Figure 2) and Falicov (2014) and analyzed using the models reviewed in Chapter 3.

TROUBLESOME TRIANGLES

Minuchin (1976) developed structural family therapy as a method to address the challenges in family life that poverty, migration, and cultural change created for people. Although his early focus was on families with a schizophrenic child and families who lived in poverty, his ideas are applicable to many family systems. As stated in earlier chapters, families, as any organization or system, have structure. Traditional Latino families are hierarchical with adults occupying the decision- and rule-making roles (executive functions); however, children also may share these functions, depending on age, birth order, and gender. For example, the "parental child" may help with chores and childrearing (Falicov 1989). In systems with clear but permeable boundaries, every family member knows his role, the rules that apply to her, and what is expected. No single family member is or feels overburdened by the expectations of others. In mutigenerational households, grandparents or other extended family members may participate in some of the childrearing functions or take care of domestic duties. In well-functioning systems, members collaborate and support one another.

Problems arise when communication is not clear or some members unwittingly or deliberately sabotage the authority of another. This may lead to the development of troublesome triangles, which can cause stress, conflict and, over time, result in more serious difficulties.

Doña Rosa, Maria, Pepe, and Susanita

Doña Rosa is an immigrant woman from El Salvador who raised two sons and a daughter alone after her husband abandoned her. She migrated to the US during the war and worked as a cook in the San Francisco Bay Area to support her children. Her sons and daughter adored her for her sacrifice, her strength, and good heart. Her daughter, Maria, married young, and both of her sons went off to college. Maria did not want her mother to live alone, worrying about her safety, since Doña Rosa lived in a high-crime area of Northern California. Doña Rosa, however, did not want to impose on the newly formed couple, especially because Pepe was Mexican origin and born in the US. Doña Rosa worried that they might have different values and he might not want to have a *suegra,* mother-in-law, living in his home. However, when Maria became pregnant, her mother acquiesced and moved in to help. Initially, both Pepe and Maria appreciated Doña Rosa's cooking and cleaning. Pepe, in particular, enjoyed coming home to warm meals and a clean house.

At first, the family functioned well; Doña Maria tried to be unobtrusive. When Susanita was born, things began to change. Both Maria and Pepe wanted to raise their children following the advice of the pediatrician and parenting books. Doña Rosa believed children should be carried all the time and fed when they cried; she was appalled that the tiny baby was sleeping alone in a crib in a separate room. She kept her views to herself but indulged her granddaughter when no one was around to see her. On several occasions, when Maria went to check on the baby at night, she found her mother asleep on the rocking chair holding the baby. Maria believed the baby should learn to "self-soothe" by being allowed to cry. Doña Rosa disagreed.

Maria talked to her mother about her wishes on several occasions but to no avail. Maria began to feel disrespected and sabotaged in her parenting by her mother. Doña Rosa was hurt that her daughter "did not trust" her parenting abilities and knowledge; moreover, she was only trying to help. Pepe felt caught between the two women and guilty that he had begun to resent his mother-in-law. The situation grew tense, and Pepe suggested to Doña Rosa that she take a vacation and go visit her relatives in El Salvador. Doña Rosa felt she was being "kicked out"; she packed her bags, kissed the baby, and left without saying goodbye. Maria was furious about her mother's drama, and Pepe felt guilty and ashamed.

After a few weeks, Maria realized how much help her mother had provided as both she and her husband had to juggle work, child care, domestic chores. They found they had no time for themselves. They both pleaded for Doña Rosa to return and negotiated some agreements about child care. Maria and Pepe realized that they were being a bit rigid with their ideas, and Doña Rosa agreed to consult with them before doing things "her way." Things may not always work out so smoothly, however, and problems with *la suegra* can create irreparable damage to a new relationship.

Edward, Luisa, and Doña Esther

Edward, a 60-year-old divorced man, met Luisa, a 49-year-old single woman, when he went to visit family in his native Honduras. Luisa was a single parent of an adult child and lived with her mother and stepfather. They began to date and Edward decided to set up household with her. He rented a spacious house; furnished it to her liking; and began to visit every few months once he retired. Edward planned to obtain a fiancé visa for Luisa in order to bring her to the United States; however, over the course of several visits, he became concerned about her "overdependence" on her mother. Edward complained that Doña Esther would arrive to their home unannounced and decide what program should be watched on TV; she also told Edward that he should not drink because it was against her religious beliefs. Edward was incensed. No woman, not even his mother, had ever told him what to do once he became a man. When he told Luisa that she should set some limits on her mother, Luisa angrily refused and began to give him "the cold shoulder."

Edward felt that Doña Esther did not trust him and that she filled Luisa's head with jealous ideas about his relationship with his ex-wife, which was amicable. Edward knew he could not give Luisa an ultimatum and have her choose between her mother and himself; but he was at his wit's end and considered ending the relationship unless things changed and Luisa became more differentiated from her mother.

Although Edward and Luisa came from similar cultural backgrounds, Edward had lived in the US for most of his adult life, and although his ex-wife had been a very strong woman, he had been the one in charge. Edward also held very traditional ideas about the position of men within the family. Luisa was his woman; he was supporting her and had created a home for both of them, which he visited regularly. He had formed a transnational relationship with her (to be discussed further in the next chapter), and he had obtained a visa for her to come to the US and decide whether or not she wanted to move there permanently with him.

His plan was to spend part of the year in the US until the violence in Honduras subsided, and then he would retire there permanently. However, he was very attached to his grandchildren and did not foresee leaving the US until the youngest, who was still a baby, was at least in elementary school. Luisa was not sure she wanted to leave her mother and join his family, which he had formed with "another woman." They had reached an impasse. Luisa felt she could not leave her mother for less than a sure thing—she did not trust that he would marry her. Similarly, he was not sure he wanted to marry a woman so dependent on her mother. At his age, he stated, he just wanted to live and let live. When he was in the US, Luisa called throughout the day wanting to know what he was doing and with whom. He felt suffocated. The troublesome triangle with Luisa's mother was threatening the viability of the relationship.

Problems that are rooted in cultural differences, communication difficulties, or relational impasses generally can be resolved utilizing most family therapy modalities as long as these are culturally attuned. However, many of the more serious challenges Latinos experience have their roots in intergenerational trauma, "What is overwhelming and unnamable is passed on to those we are closest to. Our loved ones carry what we cannot. And we do the same" (Castello 2012). For Latinos, the trauma may have its roots in the genocide of colonization, in the sequelae of the colonial period, in the Mexican-American War, in the the multiple wars and occupations of Latin America in the nineteenth and twentieth centuries, in the segregation of Mexicans and other Latinos in the US prior to the Civil Rights Movements, or in the current urban social violence resulting from decades of oppression and marginalization (Flores 2013). Such problems require a thorough evaluation of the family's structure and history, using resources and treatment approaches that are trauma informed, justice based, and culturally relevant[1].

INJUSTICE IN THE FAMILY

The major forms of family injustice among Latinos include substance misuse and abuse; family violence, including intimate partner violence (IPV); child abuse; marital rape; incest; and social violence (rape, stalking, homicide, and suicide).

SUBSTANCE ABUSE

According to a Substance Abuse and Mental Health Services Administration report (SAMHSA 2009) that utilized combined data from 2002 to 2007, an annual average of 8.3 percent (2.6 million) Latinos age 12 or older needed treatment for alcohol use in the previous year, and 3.4 percent (1.1 million) needed treatment for illicit drug use. The highest need for treatment for alcohol use was among Mexican Americans or Chicanos (9.2 percent), and the prevalence of need for treatment for illicit drug use was highest among Puerto Ricans (6.1 percent). What is most concerning is the early onset of alcohol misuse among Latino youth. An earlier report found that Latina girls were abusing alcohol and illicit drugs at rates comparable to boys and higher than female youth from other ethnic/racial groups (State of Hispanic Girls 1999). Moreover, acculturative stress and family problems constitute risk factors for adolescent substance abuse.

Significant health disparities have been found among Latino subgroups (Flores 2013). As I have noted elsewhere (Flores 2013), despite need, few Latinos receive treatment for substance abuse. Latinos also have low rates of health and mental health service utilization. The SAMHSA report also noted that *the need for treatment* for alcohol and illicit drug use as well as the receipt of illicit drug use treatment among those needing it were more likely among Latinos born in the United States than among those not born in the United States.

Alcohol remains the substance most frequently used and abused by Latinos. Among the illicit drugs, opiate and marihuana use remains high; in the past decade, there has been a rise among methamphetamine use among Latinos and Latinas, particularly US-born individuals (SAMHSA 2009). Substance misuse and abuse affects not only the user but also every member of his or her family. Substance abuse is highly correlated with all forms of family violence, including homicides and suicides.

FAMILY VIOLENCE

The National Violence Against Women Survey (2009) found that 21% of Latinas experienced physical assault at some point during their lives, and 7.9% reported having experienced an intimate partner rape. About 6% of Latina women are abused during pregnancy. In the same report, between 0.7% and 20% of Latinas report having been abused during the previous year with 23.4% reporting experiencing some form of intimate partner violence at some point in their lives. In my own investigations of Intimate Partner Violence (IPV) in both Mexico and the United States, we found similar rates of domestic violence (Flores-Ortiz, Valdez Curiel, and Andrade Palos 2002). Although some studies suggest that Latinas experience more violence than European American women, differences in rates of intimate partner violence between Latinos and non-Latinos have a tendency to disappear when factors such as age, urbanicity, and alcohol consumption are considered; in fact, socioeconomic status was found to be the most predictive of IPV among African American, European American, and Latino couples (Cunradi, Caetano, and Schafer 2002). Caetano and colleagues also found that IPV patterns do not change over time; couples that experienced violence early in their relationship continue to face multiple forms of abuse well into their midlife (Caetano, Schafer, and Cunradi 2001). The victims of this violence include not only the spouse but the children as well.

With regard to child neglect and maltreatment, during the fiscal year 2012, a nationally estimated 3.2 million children received either an investigation or an alternative response at a national disposition rate of 42.7 children per 1,000 in the population. This is a 3.5 percent increase from 2008 when an estimated 3.1 million children received a Child Protective Services response at a rate of 40.8 per 1,000 children in the population (US Department of Health and Human Services: Children's Bureau 2012). The majority of perpetrators were parents. More than three-quarters (78.3%) of child victims were neglected, 18.3 percent were physically abused, and 9.3 percent were sexually abused.

In addition, 10.6 percent of victims experienced such "other" types of maltreatment as "threatened abuse," "parent's drug/alcohol abuse," or "safe relinquishment of a newborn" (US Department of Health and Human Services: Children's Bureau 2012, 20). The same report indicates that children younger than three years of age were the most vulnerable, and Hispanic or Latino children represented 21.8 % of cases (compared to 44% White and 21% African American). Among those who were sexually abused, 26.3 percent were between 12 to 14 years of age and one-third (33.8%) were younger than nine years of age. The same report identifies adults with domestic violence and substance abuse as high risk factors for child maltreatment.

From a family systems perspective, family violence, child maltreatment, and substance abuse are interrelated problems often with the same risk factors and underlying causes; therefore, they should be treated holistically. However, these family problems are rarely treated in a coherent manner. It is the nature of health care delivery systems to treat mental health, substance abuse, and child maltreatment separately; oftentimes, families and individuals have two to three different systems or providers involved in their care provision. There is a low frequency of communication among systems or providers (Flores-Ortiz and Bernal 1990).

Causative Factors

From a family systems perspective, problems of injustice in the family must be understood and treated systemically. Families that present with such problems often face multiple stressful life events and lack more appropriate responses to deal with stressors. Likewise, it is critical to evaluate and consider the ecological factors that contribute to abuse, including poverty, social stratification, and the complex ecological niche that poor families occupy (Falicov 1989 and 2014).

In working with Latinos, as with other marginalized groups, historical legacies of injustice also must be considered, including the sequelae of colonization, which, at the macro level (or the dimension of historical realities of facts as articulated by Ivan Boszormenyi Nagy 1987), include the dependence of Latin American countries on more powerful nations and institutions (EU, USA, China, World Bank). This economic dependence often leads to pervasive conditions of poverty and corruption that adversely impact families. In addition, institutionalized racism, classism, and sexism affect the psychology of individuals and the family as a whole. In addition, historical trauma is associated with increased risk for substance misuse and abuse in both men and women (Duran and Duran 1995; Williams and Collins 1995; Williams and Mohammed 2009) as well as family injustice in all of its forms (Carrillo and Tello 2008).

The legacies of migration also need to be understood. Cultural legacies and loyalties may remain invisible yet impact how individuals feel about themselves and their place in the world. At the level of individual psychology, persistent experiences of micro- and macroaggression can result in despair, rage, and violence (Hardy and Laslofy 2005). The changes in meaning systems that accompany migration (Falicov 1998 and 2014) can evolve into family problems ranging from mild to serious in severity. Acculturative stress, especially among adolescents and young adults, can tax their coping mechanisms and result in family problems that can be viewed as disrespect (see Chapter 2) or in more serious externalizing behaviors in young people as they try to fit in or find their place in the world (Aguirre-Molina and Betancourt 2010).

Utilizing a contextual model, we can see problems of injustice as rooted in intergenerational patterns of injustice that can manifest at the level of individual psychology as

- Destructive entitlement
- Feelings of powerlessness
- Dependency
- Rage that leads to outrage

Neuroscience suggests that historical trauma compromises the neurobiology leading to problems with self-regulation. In turn, this may result in the use of substances to quiet down the internal fury (Carrillo and Tello 2008). A compromised limbic system results in poor impulse control and hyperarousal, all of which may contribute to self and other injurious behaviors (Flores 2013; van der Kolk 2005).

The impact of adverse circumstances on the family system include,

- Ungrieved losses related to migration, multigenerational trauma, or of family members due to death, incarceration, deportation, addiction
- Difficulty making commitments
- Problems with communication
- Boundary problems
- Triangulated relationships
- Substance misuse and abuse

Legacies of oppression intersect with the sequalae of more recent migrations, increasing the risk for dysfunction at the individual and family level among immigrants and children of immigrants (Flores 2013). Falicov (2014) proposes that a family's MECA map is useful in understanding why and how things can go wrong with families. Specifically, from a social justice perspective, we need to understand each family's ecological context, which is constituted by work, school, religion, and community, as well as issues related to migration and acculturation. These issues will include the losses associated with the migration (separations and reunions), trauma associated with migration, the disorienting anxieties and cultural identities related to migration, and acculturation. From a cultural diversity perspective, which refers to values and beliefs, we also need to understand the family's life cycle (constituted by ideals, meanings, timings, transitions); the family organization (whether nuclear, extended, or blended); and their patterns of communication, hierarchies, and connectedness. Such maps will address the uniqueness of each family and help us understand that which is also universal—the life cycle processes and transitions—and how these can be disrupted by migration and injustice.

LATINO FAMILIES WITH A PROBLEM OF SUBSTANCE ABUSE

Contextual family therapy views substance abuse "as rooted in social and community dynamics that impact upon the family and the person" (Bernal and Flores-Ortiz 1990, 80). These dynamics include legacies of abuse wherein substance misuse is often a multigenerational pattern. For example, grandparents may have used alcohol as a "cultural pattern" or to reduce stress or for celebrations. The adult son may have increased his alcohol consumption after migration to deal with acculturative stress, work pressures, or feelings of anxiety or depression. The US-born grandson may have begun to experiment with marijuana and alcohol and, ultimately, abuse heroin or methamphetamine to cope with marginalization, cultural identity conflicts, and a pervasive lack of belonging (Flores 2013). The grandson's addiction must be understood contextually to develop treatment strategies that are more effective (Bernal and Flores-Ortiz 1990).

Latinos show a higher incidence of substance abuse when there are ungrieved losses; these losses could be related to migration or to the substance abuse of earlier generations or to the ecological context of the family, including the erosion of community that occurs in densely populated, urban environments (Hardy and Laszloffy 2005). Substance misuse is also associated with mood and anxiety disorders, particularly among men who use substances to contain their grief or sadness (Flores 2013). In addition, contextual family therapists are concerned with the possibility that substance abuse itself may be a way of showing loyalty and concern for the family. In our early writings, Bernal and I (1990) suggested that drug abuse was a self-sacrificing behavior, which might be a family member's last ditch attempt to make family members accountable, particularly when "integrity and trustable parenting are either not available or have eroded" (81). Clearly, an alcohol-abusing father is not sufficiently available to root, enculturate, or support his children; they may, in turn, seek emotional sustenance in alcohol or other drugs, particularly if the social ecology of their community makes substances readily available and the youth have internalized stereotypes of Latinos as drinkers.

The substance-abusing family member often is the child who was maltreated, abused, or parentified. From an individual psychology perspective, she or he is seeking to soothe the fire/pain within (Carrillo and Tello 2008). The substance-abusing individual also may be the mourner or underaculturator (Sluzki 1979) in a family with a history of migration.

Many Latino families with substance abuse problems engage in a code of secrecy that helps maintain the problem. Often, this is related to concerns about social appraisal (*el qué dirán*) or to hide other problems related to substance abuse, such as family violence. In these families, dysfunction may be masked as "cultural" patterns or expectations—all men drink; drinking is central to having fun. These families may also manifest diffuse boundaries wherein it is not clear who is in charge. Indirect communication is also common and facilitates lack of accountability. US-born-or-raised children, who may be more accustomed to direct communication, may disregard messages that are not directed at them specifically. For example, parents may say "*los jóvenes no deben tomar alcohol*/young people should not drink"; to the children this may sound like an opinion and not a direct message about parental expectations. A direct statement, such as "I do not want you to drink alcohol until you are an adult," would convey a more direct rule from the parents; however, it may feel culturally incongruent to immigrants who are more comfortable with indirect messages.

As stated above, Latino families who present with substance abuse often manifest both intergenerational and contemporary patterns of loss, despair, migration-related traumas, and multiple economic and health disparities. Bernal and I (1990) discussed the case of the Soto Family. The mother, Mrs. Soto, was an immigrant from El Salvador who lost custody of her daughter Rita after she broke a jar of peppers on Rita's head when she discovered that her daughter was sexually active. In the hospital, blood tests revealed that Rita, who was 14 years old, had high levels of methamphetamine and cocaine in her system. Rita admitted the drug use to her mother's growing consternation. Mrs. Soto could not understand why her child had become a drug user.

An evaluation of the family revealed that Mrs. Soto had been a teen mother who left her two children (from different fathers) in El Salvador with her own mother when she migrated to the US to seek better economic opportunities. Rita was only 18 months old when her mother left her. In the US, Mrs. Soto partnered with a new man and had four more children. Her attempts to reunify with the children she left behind were delayed for several years. Once she was able to bring her children to the US, family reunification was fraught with difficulties as Rita and her brother considered their maternal grandmother their mother. Mrs. Soto had not visited El Salvador since she left although she sent money for the children's care; however, they felt abandoned by her and were depressed and angry. When Rita and her brother arrived in the US, their mother was expecting twins and had a five-year-old son. Rita resented her baby brother, disliked her stepfather, and was angry with her mother. Rita was nine years old. Shortly after her arrival, a family friend molested her. Her mother blamed her for the abuse and beat her. According to the children, their mother was abusive and showed them no love. Mrs. Soto argued that her older son and daughter were ungrateful and disrespectful. She denied being abusive; she explained that she had learned *a punta de palo* (due to corporal punishment) and that is why she had mended her ways and now had a relationship with a good man.

Rita's sexual behavior and drug use coincided with her mother's last pregnancy and her grandmother's arrival from El Salvador.Our contextual analysis of the case highlighted a number of multigenerational patterns: daughters having children out of wedlock and leaving them with their own mothers for care, alcohol abuse, abandonment and illegitimacy among the men, parentification of children, and extreme disciplinary practices. Also, all the women in the family were molested and blamed by family members for their own victimization. In this case, multigenerational patterns as well as the migration process, separation from family members, and involvement in the social welfare systems all compounded the family dysfunction. Rita used drugs to self-soothe and to fit in with her peer system. The therapists working with the family identified multigenerational patterns of incest, desperation, substance abuse, and abandonment that needed to be recognized in order to make changes in the present situation and prevent repetition in future generations.

From a Contextual Intergenerational Family Theory perspective, the multigenerational patterns of molestation, substance abuse, and family violence created invisible loyalties to previous generations that manifested as dysfunction. The therapists reframed Rita's "misbehavior" as an effort to make visible the hidden suffering of the women in the family. Rita's mother's violence towards her reflected her own dehumanization caused by incest and abandonment. The grandmother, mother, and Rita were connected across time by legacies of suffering and violence. To break the cycle and prevent Rita from continuing to use drugs, have unplanned pregnancies, and become an abusive mother the women needed to begin a process of healing. To become accountable to Rita and the other children both mother and grandmother needed to understand—and change—their own victimization. To prevent the boys in the family from becoming abusive the male legacies of dysfunction and abandonment also needed to be understood and changed[2].

From a narrative perspective, we can analyze this case in terms of the saturated story and the dominant narratives that impact the family negatively. Rita's saturated story was one of being unwanted. Her father did not parent her; she never knew him. Her mother left her in the care of a grandmother, who was kind but not loving given her own history of victimization. Her mother and stepfather minimized Rita's sexual abuse; instead of being supported and taken care of, she was beaten and called a whore by her mother. Mrs. Soto was influenced by a similar dominant story. Her own father sexually abused her; then he left the family. Tacitly, her mother blamed her for her father's abuse and disappearance from the family. Mrs. Soto became a teen mother and felt unwanted, unloved, unworthy. While she did not abuse alcohol or drugs, she could not parent her first two children. She left her children as a gift to her mother and fled to the US to start a new life. A grand narrative that women should sacrifice for the family also influenced Mrs. Soto's mother; she protected the men (even if they did not deserve protection), guarded secrets for the sake of *el que dirán,* and raised her grandchildren the best that she could. These grand narratives had to be deconstructed; the influence of family history, cultural norms, and adverse circumstances had to be understood in order to reconstruct and co-create with the therapists more fulfilling and healthy alternatives for all.

Ultimately, the goal of working with families where substance abuse is a problem is to focus on recovery from the addiction and from the sociocultural, political, and ecological factors that led to the onset. For Latinos, as stated above, the treatment must be attuned to the level of acculturation of the individuals who form the family, their ecological niche, and their individual psychology and family system, as well as the cultural resources they have. Treating the substance abuse without consideration of the factors that led to it is not likely to produce long-term health benefits or prevent repetition of the patterns in future generations (Bernal and Flores-Ortiz 1990).

Moreover, when girls abuse substances, it is very likely that they previously experienced some form of sexual violence; therefore, the treatment also must be trauma informed (Flores 2013). When teen boys abuse substances, it is likely they also have experienced some form of violence or denigration either in the family or society (Hardy and Laszloffy 2005). Substance abuse and the correlations of suicidality and violence are often expressions of the rage caused by marginalization, dehumanization of the losses they have experienced, and the erosion of their communities.[3]

LATINO FAMILIES WITH A PROBLEM OF VIOLENCE

Similar to Latino families with substance abuse problems, Latino families that maltreat often show legacies of abuse; that is, multigenerational patterns of domestic violence, child maltreatment, and sexual abuse as evidenced in my earlier description of the Soto family. Likewise, these families often have a higher incidence of substance misuse when compared to families where abuse is not present. At times, the dysfunction is masked as a "cultural" pattern or saturated stories—all Latino men control their women with violence; diffuse boundaries and indirect communication also are common. In cases of child maltreatment, the abused child is often the Identified Patient (as was Rita) or a parentified child.

Almeida and colleagues (1996) propose that the roots of interpersonal injustice within families and in society are located in the historical legacy of oppression and colonization, as well as the stratified caste system based on race, ethnicity, religion, sexuality, and ability instituted when the First World (Europeans) collided with the American, African, and Asian Continents. As a result of colonization, injustice was institutionalized through education, employment, and limited access to power. This institutionalization, in turn, resulted in a pyramid of oppression in which belonging and dispossession or psychological homelessness is predicated on the degree of acceptance by those in power (Flores-Ortiz 1999). Thus, it is important to understand the role of power in human relationships and, in particular, the distinction between having power and using power *over* others.

Injustice results in a hierarchy of oppression in which those with more power use it over those who are perceived to have less. At an interpersonal and intrafamilial level, power over relationships (man over woman, adults over children, employer over worker) result in a culture of terror and disrespect where abuse of power and violence can easily occur (Flores-Ortiz 1999). At an individual psychological level, oppression, particularly injustice that is racially, ethnically, gender, or class based, results in psychological homelessness (Hardy and Laszloffy 2005). As Carrillo and Tello (2008) also have noted, racism inflicts pain; discrimination creates soul wounds. Disempowerment causes pain; that pain, when compounded by loss of community and place or sense of belonging, can lead to outrage, and, in time, to rage and explosive anger. Thus, the violence engendered by racism cannot be isolated from intimate partner violence, child maltreatment, and acts of violence towards the self and others.

To understand male violence towards women of color we also need to understand men's own victimization and the gender oppression and disempowerment that is a legacy of colonization. As we have noted elsewhere (Carrillo and Tello 2008; Flores 2013), oftentimes, Latino men hurt the women and children they love because their rage cannot be directed at the perpetrators of the violence they endure. The daily indignities they face as men of color accumulate and sometimes detonate when their coping mechanisms falter, their neurobiology is compromised, or they abuse substances.

At the very least, social injustice leads to unfairness and imbalance in relationships; inauthentic connections may exist because individuals are afraid to show their true self. Others may disconnect from feelings and develop a veneer of stoicism and invulnerability. When oppression occurs, it can lead to isolation, the break up of families, or the development of unfair patterns of relationships where some members are overburdened. Injustice can also lead to the erosion of culture, particularly if dysfunctional patterns are associated with a specific group. At times, Latinas who have experienced the dark side of machismo will not date Latino men because they believe that they will be oppressive or abusive like their fathers. The pain of injustice can transform into explosive anger or rage. Intimate partner violence, child maltreatment, social violence, and self-abuse (including alcohol and other drug abuse) are some of the expressions of injustice and despair (De La Rosa, Lambert, and Gropper 1990).

Moreover, the social context of gender violence has to be considered. As Straus and Gelles (1989) have noted, in most societies, men hit because they *can*. However, when Latino and other men of color abuse those they purport to love, they do so because they can *and* because they, too, are victims of violence. Therefore, they need treatment as well as social accountability, not merely punishment (Carrillo and Tello 2008). Everyone in the family suffers when intrafamily injustice occurs. Therefore, treatment of family violence must be justice based and multimodal, often including individual, group, marital, family, and social network therapies, as well as interdisciplinary and culturally attuned.[4]

Families in which incest occurs are characterized by rigid and hierarchal gender roles that ensure male supremacy and over-privileging of male children. These families typically have diffuse boundaries and unclear, indirect patterns of communication. Such families create a climate of fear wherein women and children have no voice. Moreover, much of what occurs in the family is normalized and hidden under a mask of culture (Montalvo and Gutierrez 2001). Secrecy is labeled good behavior and family loyalty; behavioral compliance motivated by fear and terror is considered respect; and silent suffering of the abuse is reframed as loyalty (Flores-Ortiz 1993, 1995, 1997). In these families, when the perpetrator is a father or brother, and the mother does not "see" the abuse, it is likely that she also was sexually abused in her own family. Her own trauma prevents her from protecting her children or seeing the abuse when it is occurring (Flores-Ortiz 1997).

Injustice in all of its forms causes trauma. In psychiatric nomenclature, it is understood as Post-Traumatic Stress Disorder (PTSD). In the explanatory model of traditional Latinos, it may be viewed as *susto* or *espanto,* the manifestations of soul loss after a particularly difficult or traumatic incident (Flores 2013). Such trauma, then, is a causative factor for subsequent substance abuse and violence against the self and others as well as mood and anxiety disorders at the individual level. In addition to the formulations offered by the MECA, Contextual Intergenerational Family Theory, and Narrative Therapy approaches, it is critical to understand the nature of trauma from a feminist, social-justice perspective.

In addressing gender violence, the Latina Feminist Group (2001) noted that "The body speaks in languages left unread. The body encodes the *agravios*, the assaults that sometimes lead to numbness and alienation, to depression and despair, to a desire for an endless night of sleep ... women's bodies are dismembered by the ravages of institutionalized racism, by the patriarchal structures that accord privilege on the basis of gender and class, by the sexism and heterosexism that forbids love and silences desire" (Flores-Ortiz, 2001, 263).

A basic premise of feminist theory is that gender violence will not end while patriarchy prevails and until there is gender equity; likewise, the proprietary perception of women and children contributes to violence against women and children. At the root of intrafamily violence is gender oppression, distorted notions of masculinity, imbalances of power, and social injustice. Dominant ideas about gender contribute to the abuse of women as some men (and women) believe that women must be disciplined to be protected. Likewise, among Latinos and other patriarchal cultures, the cult of virginity leads to repression of female sexuality, objectification of women, and the virgin-whore dichotomy. Women are often viewed as weak, as seductresses, and unable to control their sexuality, thus, in need of "protection" from men (Flores 2013).

Across different cultures, childrearing patterns promote dependence of females and privilege male power. The boys and men are positioned as protectors (and controllers) of women. Women who contest these practices are viewed as bad women (Souza 2001). In some cultures, men are viewed as morally weaker, thus, women are made to feel responsible for controlling male sexuality. Family loyalty as a cultural dictum also silences women and prevents disclosure as does the shock of being betrayed by one's own family. How to name the unnamable? How can those who love me hurt me?[15]

In my research with college students in the late1990s (Flores-Ortiz 2003), 85 percent of the women disclosed personal experiences of physical violence in their childhood home where the father or mother was the perpetrator. One hundred women (out of a sample of 168) reported witnessing at least one incident of domestic violence between their parents. Fifty women reported being abused by a family member. Of these, 20 were

Table 2. Sequelae of Violence

SEQUELAE OF VIOLENCE	
PSYCHOLOGICAL	**ACADEMIC**
Hyper-alertness	Low academic attainment
Depression	Poor concentration
Low self-esteem	Memory lapses
Anxiety	Lack of assertiveness
Worries	Hypersensitivty
Poor concentration	Trouble finishing tasks
Difficulty trusting	Early dropouts
Difficulty forming intimate bonds	Apparent lack of interest
Difficulty with intimacy and sexuality	Reduced motivation

Adapted from: Yvette Flores-Ortiz; ed. A. Aldama, "Sequelae of Violence in Re/membering the Body: Latina Testimonies of Social and Family Violence," Violence and the Body: Race Gender and the State. Copyright © 2003 by Indiana University Press.

sexual violations. Among the sexually abused women, the age when the abuse began ranged from four to 18 years. Twenty-nine of the women reported verbal or physical attacks because of their race and witnessed violence among peers and neighbors, as well as police violence. The women manifested both psychological and academic problems, which were likely connected to their experiences of victimization (see Table 2).

Traumatic memories can manifest in the body, in the thoughts or cognitions of the victim, as well as in the emotions and interpersonal relationships.

ENCODING VIOLENCE IN THE BODY

Women's narratives often show the location of the trauma:

> *I know I am depressed because I can't stop crying. I feel tightness in my chest; I can't breathe. It's like my body remembers certain things, even though I don't want to remember, and then I try to give a name to it. Oh yes, I say to myself, this is depression. What is my body remembering? All the times he came to my room late at night, sat on the side of the bed, then climbed on top of me. At first I was scared, then I would just close my eyes and fly away. I don't consciously want to remember anything. But my body does. ... (Flores-Ortiz 2003).*

Violence in all its forms attacks the self; sexual violence leads to a mind/body split. Racial violence affects self-image; repudiation and multiple erasures also foster disconnection between mind/body and spirit (Flores 2013; van der Kolk 1994, 1997, 2005). Given the gender socialization of women, all forms of violence often lead to self-blame. Women victimized by violence often internalize blame for the abuse and "punish" themselves for their own victimization—frequently culminating in multiple forms of self-denigration, eating disorders, substance abuse, self-mutilation, myriad physical maladies, depression, high-risk behaviors (including sexual acting out), and suicide. At times, women "punish" their bodies for the assaults they have suffered; they may attack what they perceive to be the culprit—the physical attribute that called attention to themselves.

> *Here in the U S, I used to think women had more rights, but I've learned that if you are a Latina, you can't stop this stuff from happening. My boss was coming at me with compliments, or so he claimed, when I confronted him. He used to call me* "chiquita" *and tell me how beautiful my long hair was. I told him he made me feel uncomfortable. So he said I must be a feminist. Yes, I was angry, but what could I do? I needed the job. I just tried to ignore him, but the one thing I did was cut off my long hair."* Daniela, age 22

As stated, violent experiences affect the entire self and can be manifested somatically and psychologically. The long-term sequelae may compromise not only the physical and emotional health of those affected by injustice but the spirit as well

> *Who are we if not the sum total of our victimization?* Luisa, age 35

> *I feel at times that I am the walking dead. I don't believe in God, how could a God, whether Christian or something else allow little children to be hurt by those who are supposed to care for them? My body will walk the earth until I die, but my spirit left a long time ago.* Tina, age 35

> *The spark of life grows ever dimmer. I was once a vibrant child, a happy little girl. Then her assaults began. I could feel myself shrinking. I may be over 50 years of age, but a hurt little girl lives inside of me. She is the only part of me that is alive.* Se me fue el espíritu desde hace tiempo. Olga, age 55

As noted elsewhere (Flores-Ortiz 1997), battered women and sexually abused children are similar to survivors of state terror and prisoners of war. The process of victimization attempts to rob the individual of her will, her sense of self, and her ability to control even basic physical functions. The victim's thoughts and behaviors are subject to the control of the more powerful perpetrator (Herman 1992). The perpetrator isolates the family through rigid control, often forbidding the women and girls from going anywhere without him, even visiting their own families. Michael Johnson (2008) labels such perpetrators *intimate terrorists* because they use tactics similar to those utilized in warfare to instill terror and gain control of the enemy.

In these families, boys often are enlisted or coerced to function as enforcers of discipline and control of sisters. The wives/mothers in such families may be unable to protect the children due to their own victimization as battered women or victims of sexual abuse themselves. In the climate of fear created by the perpetrator and often supported by social institutions, women and children suffer violations silently or turn against one another. Women may blame the girls for "the seduction of the husband." Nuclear- and extended family members may collude in the maintenance of the abuse "as love is confused with sex, loyalty with obligation, and respect with silent endurance of violations" (Flores-Ortiz 1997, 57).

TREATMENT CONSIDERATIONS

In the treatment of IPV, the focus should be on why men abuse, not why women stay in unjust relationships. Such a question is blaming and it de-contextualizes the experience of abuse. In cases of IPV and sexual violence, community accountability is essential. Services are needed for women and men who are victims and/or perpetrators. Ancillary services for men who batter and abuse sexually are essential to help the perpetrator become accountable. Once the perpetrator of violence becomes accountable, the family can be treated together (Flores-Ortiz, Esteban, and Carrillo 1994).[6] From a Contextual Intergenerational Family Theory perspective, the treatment includes reconstructive dialogues (Flores-Ortiz 1998) to foster accountability among those who have hurt, breaking the silence for those who have been injured, and rebalancing the relational scales to prevent the repetition of these patterns in future generations.

From a Narrative Therapy perspective that is rooted in social justice, the path to healing entails finding meaning among those who have been hurt. An important step is externalizing the blame, giving testimony to break the silence and, thereby, contesting, challenging, and holding accountable both the perpetrators and those who did not protect. Cultural narratives of victimization and dominant stories of suffering and victimhood must be re-scripted. By building a community of support, the larger society collaborates in the healing. As stated earlier, the Dulwich Center advocates for the use of humor, storytelling, and (re)connecting to ancestral culture in order to heal. "Remembering the body" is often the first step to integrating body-mind-spirit, which is crucial to heal from trauma.

My work with survivors of incest and marital rape focuses on healing the trauma through an integrative therapy of bodywork, art, and feminist relational therapy (Flores-Ortiz 1997). Whether in individual or family therapy, the woman is helped to heal the body, mind, and soul; rebalance relationships with family members; and externalize the blame. Incest, in particular, creates soul wounds that interfere with a woman's enjoyment of her body and, over time, may contribute to physical illness (Flores-Ortiz 1997; Flores 2013; van der Kolk 1994).

"Becky"

In my work with "Becky," an incest survivor, we focused on releasing the shame associated with sexual abuse. In addition, through ritual and artwork, she was able to express her grief, shame, horror, and guilt. Over time, she was able to contextualize those who abused her and re-script her story of victimization into one of survival (Flores-Ortiz 1997).

> *I am far more than the paintings I give birth to out of my pain. I don't want to be remembered as an incested woman, a survivor of family violence. I want to be remembered for the totality of my being, for everything I have done, not for what was done to me.*
>
> *I finally inhabit my body. I feel the beating of my heart, I know what I am thinking in the moment, I can translate my emotions, and I have conquered fear. I can say I am no longer afraid to love, to make love, to be touched. But more importantly, while I cannot recover the innocence he robbed, I got back my soul.*
>
> *Joyfulness, playfulness, aliveness have replaced depression, dissociation and despair, pretty cool huh?* "Becky," age 29

Male incest survivors also struggle with questions about their masculinity if the perpetrators were male and with the minimization of their suffering by others if the perpetrators were female. Latino boys and young men, who were victims of sexual abuse by women and tell their fathers, often encounter congratulatory responses as if the boys or young men had been willing sexual partners of the perpetrators. They are often filled with shame and are silenced. Given the likelihood of homophobic responses to sex with men, males often are silenced if the perpetrators were male for fear that they will be considered gay. In many families, unless the boys were very young and the perpetrators were not family members, sexual victimizations are rarely reported or the children rarely given enough support. Many Latino families hide such victimizations for fear of *el que dirán* under the guise of protecting the children from shame and humiliation. The implicit message the victims receive is that they are somehow complicit or to blame for the victimization.

Thus, recovery from incest and IPV is a life-long struggle; the survivor must learn to identify and avoid the triggers to PTSD symptomatology. She or he must learn to live with his/her story and transform it. Reconnecting to the body, healing the spirit and emotions, advocacy, and breaking the silence are important paths to healing. Family accountability and social support are essential for long-term recovery.

HOMEWORK ASSIGNMENT

- Develop a MECA family map.
    - What is the ecological context of your family?
    - What are salient migration and acculturation issues?
    - What do you see as the most pronounced patterns of injustice affecting your family?
    - What is the life cycle of your family of origin? (Note that your family may be in several stages simultaneously—school-age children and launched offspring.)
    - What are the most important values and beliefs evident in your family?
    - What is your current family organization? What was it while you were growing up?
    - How would you describe your family's patterns of communication?
- Identify injustice or dysfunctional patterns in your family of origin.
- Once you have completed your genealogy, identify patterns of injustice that repeat over generations (i.e., substance misuse or abuse, IPV, divorce, abandonment).
- Reflecting on your family's history, what hypotheses do you have regarding these patterns of injustice? What may be some causative or contributing factors?
- Given your family history, what is your dominant story?
- What cultural, gender, and social scripts currently influence you and your family?
- What may be some cultural grand narratives that affect you in terms of your gender and sexuality and class position?
- Reflecting on your family history, what are the sources of resiliency and strength?

ENDNOTES

1. For an excellent formulation of working with Latino families in therapy, see Celia Falicov, 2014, *Latino Families in Therapy* (second edition), NY Guilford Press.
2. For a full discussion of the case and the course of treatment, see G. Bernal, and Y. Flores-Ortiz, 1990, "Contextual Family Therapy with Adolescent Drug Abusers," in C. Todd (Ed.), *Family Therapy Approaches with Adolescent Substance Abusers*, New York: Allyn and Bacon, 70–92.
3. See Ken Hardy and Tracy Lazloffy, 2005, *Teens who Hurt: Clinical Implications to Break the Cycle of Adolescent Violence*, New York: Guilford Press, and Yvette Flores, 2013, *Chicana and Chicano Mental: Alma, Mente y Corazón*, Tucson: University of Arizona Press.

4. See Y. Flores-Ortiz, 1999. "Migracion, Identidad y Violencia/Migration, Identity and Violence." in M. Mock, L. Hill, and D.Tucker (Eds.), *Breaking Barriers: Psychology in the Public Interest*, Sacramento, CA: California Psychological Association, 46–59.

   For examples of treatment of families with problems of violence, see Y. Flores-Ortiz, 1999, "From Margin to Center: Family Therapy with Latinas," in M. Flores and G. Carey (Eds.), *Family Therapy with Hispanics*, Boston: Allyn & Bacon, 5976; Y. Flores-Ortiz, 1993, "La Mujer y La Violencia: A Culturally Based Model for the Understanding and Treatment of Domestic Violence in Chicana/ Latina Communities," in N. Alarcón et al. (Eds.), *Chicana Critical Issues,* Berkeley: Third World Press, 1, 169–182; Y. Flores-Ortiz, M. Esteban, R. and Carrillo, 1994, "La Violencia en la Familia: Un Modelo Contextual de Terapia Intergeneracional," *Revista Internamericana de Psicología*, v. 28, (2), 235–250; Y. Flores-Ortiz, 1998, "Fostering Accountability: A Reconstructive Dialogue with a Couple with a History of Violence," in T. Nelson, and T. Trepper (Eds.), 1998, *101 More Interventions in Family Therapy*, N.Y.: Haworth Press, 389–396,
5. For further elaboration of these ideas, see Y. Flores-Ortiz, 2004,"Domestic Violence in Chicano Families," in Roberto Velazquez, L. Arellano, and B. McNeill (Eds.), *The Handbook of Chicana/o Psychology and Mental Health*, New Jersey: Lawrence Erlbaum Associates, 267–284; Y. Flores-Ortiz, 2005, "Why did he want to hurt me: all I ever did was love him?: Understanding Sexual Violence in Latino Marriages," in E. Buchwald, P. R. Fletcher, and M. Roth (Eds.), *Transforming a Rape Culture* (second edition), Minneapolis: Milkweed Editions, 129–138; and Y. Flores-Ortiz, 2001, *La Tra(d)icion. Latina Feminist Group. Telling to Live: Latina Feminist Testimonios,* Duke University Press, 204–206.
6. For a different modality of treatment, see Cloe Madanes, 1990, *Sex, Love, and Violence: Strategies for Transformation*, NY: Norton and Norton.

CHAPTER 5

POLITICS, POLICIES, AND THE FORMATION OF TRANSNATIONAL FAMILIES

Scholars have described the process of transnational migration as one entailing "ambiguous losses and gains[1]" (Falicov 2014). Leaving the homeland, regardless of the type of migration, results in losses, grief, and mourning for migrants as they leave behind loved ones, networks of support, and their familiar context and ecological niche. As stated in earlier chapters, post-migration adjustment is facilitated or hindered by the degree of reception of the receiving country. Every immigrant to the United States has encountered particular circumstances and varying degrees of acceptance that determined, in part, their structural integration to the United States.

Latinos have had a particular history with regard to migration. In the 1840s, the Treaty of Guadalupe Hidalgo incorporated Mexicans into the US (Rosales 1991); they did not migrate. As Antonio Burciaga (1992) stated, "We did not cross the border; the border crossed us." This border became an open wound that many would later traverse by foot, water, and air to rejoin family members, flee political oppression, escape wars and revolutions, and seek better economic opportunities. At various points in US history, policies have welcomed Mexican migrant labor (i.e., the Bracero program, 1942–1964)[2] but disinvited them to stay after their *brazos* (arms and labor) were no longer needed. Some remained and adjusted their status; others left and returned to Mexico creating a legacy of transnational migration. *El Sueño Americano* (the American dream) of greater economic prosperity offered a path out of poverty for rural Mexicans who imagined a better life for their families if they sought work in the North. *El Norte* became the Promised Land. Thus, since the 1960s, millions of Mexicans have continued the journey north, many to reunify with relatives who had obtained legal status for them while others crossed the border without documentation and became unauthorized migrants.

In the 1990s, Mexican migration to the US increased; some attribute this increase to the Free Trade Agreement (NAFTA), which resulted in increases in unemployment and reduced agricultural production in Mexico[3]. As a result, official Mexican government data indicates over 12 million of its citizens live abroad, mostly in the US. Of these, 45% are women and 55% are men (Rivera Heredia et al. 2014).

Central Americans, particularly from El Salvador, Nicaragua, and Honduras, migrated in large numbers to the US in the mid- and late-twentieth century as a result of civil wars, natural disasters, and the legacies of US intervention in the region that destabilized economies, pushing hundreds of thousands into poverty and despair (Mahler 2006). Most recently, the proliferation of drug cartels and the violence attributed to gangs, such as the *Mara Salvatrucha* (MS–13) and their rival, M–18, have led to mass migrations of Hondurans, Salvadorans, and Guatemalans, many of them children (Savenije 2007; Wolf 2012). These unaccompanied minors recently have been the focus of significant media attention and are challenging existing US immigration policies under the Obama Administration (Restrepo and Garcia 2014).

As a result of the continuing influx of Latino immigrants to the US, families may be formed by transnational migrants from different countries and by US-born Latinos and migrants who are authorized or unauthorized; Latinos of different generations may partner and have children who may hold varying degrees of identification with their Latino ethnocultural roots. Other families have mixed status; some members are US citizens or authorized residents while others are undocumented. Others are of mixed race as Latinos partner with African Americans, Middle Easterners, Asian Americans, South Asian Indians, and European Americans.

This chapter focuses on the impact of immigration policies on Latinos from various national origins. First, I examine the pursuit of the American dream and the push-and-pull factors that result in the migration of men and women from Latin America. Second, I examine the sequelae of deportations and exclusions on Latino families and the forced formation of divided families due to mixed status. This section is followed by a discussion of the impact of microaggressions and macroagressions on children and youth in mixed status families. The last section offers an analysis of rooting and belonging in the context of being positioned as an "other."

MIGRATION AND FAMILY LIFE: WHY MIGRANTS LEAVE AND WHY THEY DO (NOT) RETURN

Today, around 214 million people, approximately 3 percent of the world's population, live outside of their country of birth. Stiglitz, Cortina, and Ochoa-Reza, (2013,,xv) document that women and girls account for half of international migrants, and 16 percent are under the age of 20. Moreover,

> *South-south migration is now as frequent as south-north migration has been in the past, and while 97 percent of the world's population does not move, migration is a global phenomenon that touches millions of lives, including many of those of haven't themselves migrated (Stiglitz, Cortina, and Ochoa-Reza 2013, xv).*

As stated earlier, many factors motivate a migration away from one's homeland[4]. There are factors, such as unemployment and poverty, war, social unrest, and political or religious persecutions, that push people out of their countries. There are also pull factors that "invite" people to migrate to particular countries, such as the United States. Typically, the pull factors are the expectation of work and improved economic opportunities. Family reunification is also a motivator for transnational migration. Likewise, migrants often have both "official stories" and the more covert or secret reasons for leaving.

My father left his homeland at age 19 after his mother died in order to seek better economic opportunities and, thereby, help support his younger siblings. This was the official story. However, the unofficial story was that his father's philandering and his bringing a young mistress to raise his orphaned children outraged my father. Thus, my father left Costa Rica for Panama to seek work and escape an untenable situation. He was also following the legacy of his paternal and maternal grandfathers who had migrated from Spain and China, respectively, and partnered with indigenous women, thereby, contributing to the racial tapestry that became my family of origin. Although he migrated to work and support his sisters, in Panama, my father met my mother. He became her protector and provider for her two young sons, the product of her failed first marriage, thus, adding a layer of responsibility to his life that he had not anticipated upon migration. Although he now had a woman and children to support, he continued to help his sisters financially and emotionally.

This is often the experience of young men who migrate alone seeking better economic opportunities to help their parents. Eventually, they form their own families, adding to the financial responsibilities that propelled their migration. The departure of sons and brothers affects the entire family left behind. Thus, drawing on the experiences of high sender communities of Mexico, Rivera Heredia and colleagues (2014) argue that migration cannot be considered an individual process as it affects all aspects of the private and public lives of relatives, neighbors, and friends. Due to the reliance on remittances sent from the US, many Mexican communities depend on the migration of the young and able-bodied to subsist since not only do remittances support people but they may also contribute to the infrastructure of the town[5].

Why Men Migrate

The majority of Mexican men who come to the US from rural communities do so to improve the financial situation of their families that they left behind (Flores, Rivera-Lopez, and Brazil-Cruz 2014; Rivera Heredia et al. 2014). In our studies of the impact of migration on Mexican men's mental health and family functioning, we found that the primary reason for migration of the Mexican men interviewed was providing for their parents and siblings. Most had migrated in their late teens and had male relatives who had migrated before them—most notably, cousins and uncles. Most of the men had been unable to return to visit their families and had endured losses due to death, long-term separation, and failure to attain the American dream. The majority were unauthorized migrants who had risked border crossings multiple times in order to visit their parents in the first few years after their migration. They worked to send back remittances. A few had met and married women from their *ranchos* and left them behind when they returned, thus, creating transnational families. Some returned annually for visits; the women became pregnant during these visits, thereby increasing the economic demands on the migrant man. The men also worked then to send money back so that their wives could save to build a home for him and the family upon his return.

However, after the attacks of September 11, 2001, and the increased militarization of the US-Mexico border, many of these men were unable to return to Mexico for fear of the more treacherous journey across the desert and the increased risk of detention and deportation. In some cases, the women made the journey north to join their husbands, leaving their children in their parents' care. In the US, both partners worked to support themselves and the children left behind. For the men, having new family responsibilities created a burden of guilt as they were less able to help their parents—the original purpose for their migration. These couples often had children in the US; thereby creating mixed status families. The younger children were US citizens; the parents, unauthorized immigrants who lived in fear of detection and deportation. The older children were in Mexico separated from their families and siblings. All dreamed of an eventual family reunification, which, if it came to pass, was fraught with conflict and anxiety as will be discussed later in this chapter.

In some cases, the wife and children migrated together to join the male migrant. As the children grew up, they faced the challenges of being unauthorized, as well. These young people lived in the shadows, unable to obtain driver's licenses (a rite of passage for many adolescents), work, or obtain financial aid to attend college. Thus, immigrant parents often saw their dreams of affording their children a better life through education thwarted by immigration policies and their decision to bring the children to the US without proper documentation. It was not until the Development, Relief, and Education of Alien Minors Act (DREAM Act) was created to give unauthorized child immigrants to the US an opportunity to enlist in the military, go to college, or have a path to citizenship that some of their situations improved.

Don Alberto

For Don Alberto, a 45-year-old Mexican immigrant who had spent 28 years of his life in the US, the primary reason for migrating was to help his family. He was the eldest of 11 siblings. For the first few years post-migration, he lived in central California; he worked in the fields and returned to Mexico during the off-season. He did not seek a wife or partner because "his mission was to work to help out" his parents. He did not want to be "side-tracked" or add other responsibilities that would deter him from his original goal of building his parents a more livable home. Each time he visited Mexico he brought money and some materials to expand his parents' modest home. Eventually, he built a house with four rooms so that his parents could have their own room, his seven brothers could share two rooms, and his three sisters could share the remaining room. Over time, his siblings married and formed families of their own. Don Alberto indicated that he discouraged his brothers from migrating; he sent extra money when he could to make sure they remained in Mexico to avoid the suffering he endured—the loneliness away from family, the lack of well-paid work opportunities, and the temptations to escape into alcohol and drug use.

In one of the visits to his *rancho* in rural Michoacán, Don Alberto met Alicia, a woman 15 years his junior. They fell in love and married. Don Alberto continued the migration to California annually, now supporting a wife in addition to his parents, Two years after they married, Marisol was born. As their daughter grew older and his visits became less frequent, his wife insisted on joining him. Alicia and Marisol crossed the border without inspection and the family reunified. Don Alberto commented that since their arrival, his life had become more stressful. His wife had to go to work as he could not afford a house for them solely on his income. He had rented a room with a number of other migrant men prior to his wife's arrival. However, he could not bring her and their 13-year-old daughter to live with a group of men. As a result of both partners having to work, Don Alberto felt the quality of his family life had diminished. They had little time to spend together.

Now, his worries also included concerns about Marisol's education as she struggled to learn English and perform at grade level in a different educational system. Doña Alicia worried about her daughter's future and was committed to finding a way to support her academically so that she could succeed. Both she and her husband were aware that Marisol would face significant challenges as an unauthorized person in the US but felt the sacrifice was worth the hardship. They wanted the best for Marisol. Don Alberto, however, was distressed about the added responsibility and felt guilty that he now had to focus on his own family and less on his parents who still depended on him for support.

Given the limited work opportunities available to unauthorized male immigrants, the American dream becomes illusive. For those men who migrate alone and are young, sadness and loneliness can lead them to substance abuse. For older men, alcohol may also be an outlet to manage the grief and losses that accompany migration. One of our male research participants noted that sometimes they drink too much and do not have enough money to send their wives; then, they make up stories that work was slow or they were not paid in order to explain why they could not send money back that particular time (Flores, Rivera-Lopez, and Brazil-Cruz 2014).

Most of the men dreamt about eventually going back to their home and their families. Few realize that dream voluntarily. Many are deported only to try to return promptly to continue the pursuit of a better life. With each migration, debt is incurred both in the US and in their country of origin as few men have the resources to pay for the passage. Often, they borrow from relatives in the US who have to pay *the coyote* (human trafficker) for the transport of the migrant. Thus, in the first few months in the US, men work to generate the income needed to pay back the debt. Many men and their families in the country of origin spend years in debt because of the increased costs of migration to the US.

As noted elsewhere, male migration to the US creates risk factors for substance abuse and mood and anxiety disorders, causing disruptions in family life on both sides of the border (Falicov 2014; Flores 2013). Men we have interviewed refer to these risks factors as the "emotional costs of migration" (Flores, Rivera-Lopez, and Brazil-Cruz 2014).

As shown in Don Alberto's story, some of the stress men experience post-migration is related to their wives' entry into the labor force.

In our study of rural Mexican men in Central California, we interviewed two men whose wives had "changed dramatically" after they began to work. One recounted how his wife began to socialize with co-workers after work; she began to go out dancing to a nearby town while he stayed home with their two children and eventually began an extramarital affair that resulted in their separation. This man blamed the end of his marriage on his wife's encounter with temptation. He blamed himself, in part, for not being able to afford a life style that precluded her having to go to work.

However, not all couples find family reunification or transnational relationships fraught with conflict and challenges. Hirsh's (2003) study of transnational couples in Atlanta, Georgia, addresses the ways in "gender structures and is in turn structured by transnational social ties" (17). Hirsh noted how both men and women understand the gender differences in the US and Mexico and how gender roles are negotiated to deal with those differences. She introduces the term '"companionate marriages" to describe the type of bond created by transnational couples to maintain both emotional and sexual intimacy despite the distance that separates them. These bonds are based on mutual respect and trust. Women who are left behind focus on raising the children and keeping the dream of *familia* alive for the benefit of the husband and their children. While the man is away, they are de facto authority and decision makers. Women in our studies often refer to this as "borrowed power," which they surrender when the husband arrives for a visit (Flores and Valdez Curiel 2003).

In the US context, once reunified, some couples work to address gender inequalities that may have been more culturally appropriate in their town of origin but are not functional in their new social context. In my own work (Flores-Ortiz 1993), Mexican immigrant women found life in the US to be more amenable to shared decision making and to greater voices in their marriages. Husbands adjusted to relationship changes; although men expressed some regret at their loss of power within the home, some welcomed their wives' increasing independence. A few men feared that the increased independence afforded by having their own earned income would result in the wives leaving them. A man, whose wife began to jog, feared that one day she would start running away from him and never turn back (Flores-Ortiz 1993).

Why Women Migrate

The increase in female migration to the US is primarily associated with escape from poverty, situations of family or social violence, or to reunify with family members already in the US (Flores and Valdez Curiel 2009). Central American female migration increased during the civil wars of El Salvador and Nicaragua as well as the repression against indigenous groups in Guatemala and Mexico. In some of my earlier writings (Flores-Ortiz 2002 and 2003; Flores 2012), I examined the push-and-pull factors that bring women to the US. The increased migration of Mayan women from the Yucatan Peninsula of Mexico, for example, has been labeled "the new Mayan route." Many of these women escape persecution by government officials and the military and seek political asylum in the US. Many left children behind in hopes of reunifying with them in the future. Many experience rape and physical abuse during the journey, arriving to the US with extreme trauma. Others migrate to flee persecution or join their husbands in the US, who fled before them, or both.

For Guatemalans and other Central American migrants, the journey entails negotiating multiple borders and facing detection, detention, and deportation back to their countries, as well as being robbed, beaten, and raped by Mexican police, gang members, and even other migrants[6]. Many women migrate to escape family violence only to encounter equally adverse conditions in the US.

Maritza's Story

Maritza is the third of seven children born to a *mestizo* family in Chiapas, Mexico. She described a childhood filled with violence and despair. Her parents were very poor; an older brother left for Mexico City to work when he was still a child. An older sister also had left the family to seek work; consequently, her mother relegated household chores to Maritza from a very early age as she was the oldest girl at home. She felt that her mother mistreated her for being female. She beat her when the chores were not done to her satisfaction. Maritza had to prepare meals, take care of her younger siblings, and remain in the home. She was not allowed to go outside to play or to attend school. Her younger brothers worked in the fields, and she had to cook for them and wash their clothes. Her parents reportedly told her that her place was at home because she was a girl.

When Maritza was seven or eight, she does not recall exactly, her 17-year-old brother, who lived in Mexico City, began to sexually abuse her when he came home on vacation. He also beat her whenever he felt like it. When she complained to her parents about the physical violence, she was told that because he was older he had the right "to discipline" her. She did not tell her parents about the sexual abuse. She feared they would not believe her and beat her "for lying." Her parents favored their sons over their daughters.

The first time her brother sexually abused her he had come for a visit and began to rub himself against her back. Because she told him to stop, he hit her on the head with a belt buckle. He gave her a choice: to beat her or rape her. She began to cry and he raped her and then beat her. Thereafter, whenever he came home from the city, he brought her pretty dresses and had her put them on. He would then remove the dresses and rape her. He sodomized her, made her perform oral sex, and vaginally penetrated her on multiple occasions. Maritza stated that her spirit left her body when he did these things. She dissociated. Over time, she became increasingly despondent. She considered suicide many times. As she grew older, she began to experience night terrors, episodes of severe anxiety, which she did not know were symptoms of trauma. She migrated to the United States at age 19 to escape her abusive family. She began to work and tried to put the past behind her. However, she eventually became involved with a man who drank to intoxication and physically and verbally abused her. She had a daughter Kristina with him but eventually left him due to his abuse and infidelity. He flaunted his affairs and brought his lovers to the house for her to feed them. After being alone for a few years, Maritza then became involved with another man who also drank and verbally abused her. She had her daughter Celeste with him. Neither man provided financially for the girls.

Maritza worked long hours to provide for her daughters; thus, she relied on Kristina to take care of the home and help with Celeste. Economic circumstances and her position as an unauthorized migrant forced her to repeat child-rearing patterns that she had endured and abhorred. Kristina felt it was unfair to have to be a mother to her younger sister and began to rebel. She cut school and spent time with gang-involved youth. Maritza indicated that she did not know what to do. Kristina was becoming increasingly rebellious. One day she saw that her daughter was sending nearly nude photos of herself to her boyfriend. Maritza stated that she lost control; as she began to hit her daughter, Maritza screamed and cried without being able to stop. She saw her mother in herself and wanted to die.

Because of this incident, Maritza was arrested and lost custody of her daughters when school officials reported Maritza's bruises as possible child abuse. When she was jailed, she was evicted, lost her two jobs, and became homeless. Child Protective Services (CPS) became involved and her daughters were placed in foster care until Maritza completed a treatment program and found suitable housing. Maritza stated that CPS referred her to individual and family therapy. In the course of therapy, she disclosed her childhood physical and sexual abuse. This began a gradual healing process. She and her daughters spent a year in individual and family therapy and reported being grateful that due to CPS "and God" her daughter Kristina had begun to recover. Kristina finished high school and began to attend a local junior college.

After her arrest, Maritza lost custody of Kristina for 18 months and of Celeste for 10 months. These were her darkest days, she indicated. Celeste was only a year old and developed attachment problems. Although Celeste is improving with therapy, Maritza feels that her younger daughter continues to have problems. Maritza is devastated that her loss of control affected her daughters and caused a long separation. She wept as she confided that she had come to the US to escape violence only to encounter more and to become violent herself. She had wanted, instead, to end the generational cycle of violence in which she grew up. She fled her family to escape their violence and found herself hurting her daughters. With the aid of therapy, she came to understand that the verbal abuse, the physical violence, and the sexual abuse she endured affected her emotionally and behaviorally. She carries within her, her own mother's words that she is useless, worthless, good for nothing. She understands that her involvement with abusive men is a result of her childhood victimization and lack of self-esteem. She wants to make sure her daughters do not have her same fate. Yet, she continued to become involved with men who did not treat her well.

However, because of her arrest on child abuse charges, Maritza is on deportation proceedings. She fears that if she is deported, she will lose her daughters forever. She does not want her daughters to experience the poverty in which she grew up. She cannot return to her family as the abuse from them will continue. She has no one else in Mexico who can help her. She would have to leave her daughters, first, because Kristina is attending college in the US, and, second, because Celeste's father cannot be found in order to obtain his consent for their daughter to leave the country. If Maritza is forced to return to Mexico, either Kristina will have to take care of Celeste or her youngest child will, once again, enter the foster care system.

Many immigrant women experience the same circumstances as Maritza, others are able to thrive and form functional families. However, living in the shadows due to unauthorized status increases the risk of family separation; it creates a climate of anxiety and fear for many immigrants with a pervasive sense of a lack of belonging and rootedness for their children, which can manifest as adolescent acting out as in Kristina's case.

RETURNING "HOME"

When we asked migrants to identity the barriers to returning home, most stated that they could not leave until they were financially solvent, have enough savings to live better in their country of origin, or when the political situation in their country had improved (Flores, Rivera-Lopez, and Brazil-Cruz 2014). For most, returning home becomes complicated when they have children in the US, become ill, or cannot go back due to increased violence in their homelands. Most immigrants who migrated as adults experience the nostalgia of home as discussed in earlier chapters. They may experience psychological homelessness (Hardy and Laszloffy 2005) and feel they are neither "from here nor there," a situation also experienced by their US-born-or-raised children, which will be discussed later in this chapter.

In her study of Mexican returnees to rural Michoacán, Cervantes Pacheco (2014) found that most men hope to return to the US. Many of the men were deported; sometimes, they were stopped for minor traffic violations or driving without a license or after a car accident. Unable to pay for an immigration attorney, they were deported after days, weeks, and, sometimes, months of detention and frequent maltreatment. They returned to a Mexico that was unfamiliar and to a social context that resented, devalued, and, at times, envied them. They relived the stages of migration discussed in earlier chapters but this time without hope of improving their life circumstances. Some were able to establish businesses; however, most returned to their country to struggle economically to support their families. This situation often resulted in depression. In instances when the family remained in the US, the women had to work to support themselves and send remittances to the husband until he could "get back on his feet."

The formation of transnational families as a result of migration and deportation back to the country of origin complicates the family's ability to negotiate life cycle stages and to support the children emotionally while, at the same time, perpetuating the legacy of migration (Cervantes, Mejia, and Guerrero Mena 2010; Falicov 2014).

IMPACT OF IMMIGRATION POLICIES ON LATINO FAMILIES

The Illegal Immigration Reform and Illegal Immigrant Responsibility Act of 1996 (Cervantes, Mejia, and Guerrero Mena 2010; Hing 2004) adversely affected mixed status families. These are families in which one or more children or a spouse are either citizens or legal residents and others are unauthorized. Individuals who entered the US without inspection were criminalized. In various states, drivers' licenses were no longer obtainable without proof of legal residency or citizenship. After 2001, The Patriot Act allowed for the mandatory detention of "certified aliens," that is, individuals who could not produce documentation verifying legal residency or citizenship (Sinnar 2003). Immigrants who might have lived for decades in the US were subject to detection and detention. Workers became more vulnerable to exploitation as fines were issued to employers if they hired undocumented workers. So the immigrants were paid "under the table" without any benefits or fair compensation. Many immigrants lost well-paying jobs in construction and other industries if they lacked legal status or a work permit. With the loss of these jobs came loss of health insurance benefits. Many Latinos also lost their homes as they could no longer afford mortgages.

As noted in the American Psychological Association's Presidential Task Force Report on Immigration (APA 2011), 79 percent of the children of undocumented immigrant adults are citizens as the 14th Amendment grants them automatic citizenship (Passel and Taylor 2010, cited in APA). Moreover, more than 4 million citizen children live in homes with undocumented parents, and another 1.1 million children are undocumented themselves. According to Passel and Taylor (2010), most immigrant children live in mixed citizen status families whereby some members are citizens and others are not. This situation creates complicated dynamics and ambivalent relationships within the family, according to Carola Suárez-Orozco and her colleagues (2011). Celia Falicov describes how the varying levels of access family members may have depending on their immigration status contribute to family conflict. Moreover, Yoshikawa (2011) has noted that although children who grow up in homes with undocumented parents are more likely to live in two-parent families, they are also more likely to live in poverty because their parents work in poorly remunerated and precarious jobs. As a result, many of these citizen children are less likely to be enrolled in programs that could help to foster their early learning (e.g., preschool, Head Start) or to have access to health care (De la Torre et al. 2010; Yoshikawa 2011). Thus, mixed status contributes to maintaining health disparities among Latino groups.

With the passing of the Patriot Act and subsequent Homeland Security measures, life for mixed status families became more stressful due to economic uncertainty and fear of apprehension. US-born-or-raised children lived in fear of their parents being detained and deported, particularly as Immigration and Custom Enforcement (ICE) raids became commonplace in Latino neighborhoods. Chui et al. (2009), in a report of the Cardozo Immigration Law clinic titled "Constitution on ICE," document that during the last two years of the Bush administration, "(ICE) vastly expanded its use of home raid operations as a method to locate and apprehend individuals suspected of civil immigration law violations" (1). ICE officials indicated that these raids could be done without a warrant, but any entries into homes required the informed consent of residents.

> *However, frequent accounts in the media and in legal filings have told a similar story of constitutional violations occurring during ICE home raids—a story that includes ICE agents breaking into homes and seizing all occupants without legal basis (Chui et al. 2009, 1).*

Other raids consisted of entering job sites in factories, construction, and agricultural fields to demand proof of legal residency. At times, ICE agents waited outside people's homes to detain them as happened to the Arias family of Sacramento, California.

The Arias Family

Luis and Angela Arias met in the US; they both had migrated in their youth to join their parents, unauthorized immigrants, who sent for their children once they established themselves in northern California. Luis and Angela met at the restaurant where she worked. They married and had three children. Luis worked in construction and with both of their salaries they were able to buy a home. Their son, Gabriel, was a sophomore in high school when ICE knocked at their door one morning. Lolita, an eighth grader, had been braiding her seven-year-old sister Elena's hair when she heard a commotion and her mother scream. She ran to the door and saw three men had thrown her father on the floor; their mother was begging for an explanation. Gabriel was terrified. An ICE agent reportedly told the parents, "I'm gonna be nice, so one of you has to come with me right now; the other can stay until you find someone to take care of your kids but must turn yourself in within a month. You are illegal and gotta go back." This is how Gabriel and his siblings learned that their parents were not US citizens. Luis told the agents he would go with them. He was handcuffed and arrested. Within 72 hours, he was back in Mexico, a country he had left at age 15.

In the following month, Angela struggled to control her feelings of devastation and began to sell everything the couple owned; with the help of her legal-resident sister and parents, she rented out her home as she hoped she and her family could be back in a short time. Angela arranged for her two older children to go live with her sister until the end of the school year. Prior to the end of the month she was given, she signed a "voluntary departure" and returned to Guanajuato, Mexico, with Elena. Her husband had been unable to find work in Jalisco, his hometown, and joined her in Guanajuato, where her maternal grandparents lived. As soon as school was out for the year, Gabriel and Lolita left for Mexico. Gabriel had been an A student and basketball player. In Mexico, school officials told him that he would have to enter the sixth grade because he was not fully literate in Spanish. He stopped going to school and became suicidal. The couple's relatives in the US sent them money to pay for psychiatric treatment for Gabriel.

Prior to her departure, Angela had contacted an immigration lawyer who began the process of petitioning for their return. Angela's mother was a legal resident with a chronic and debilitating illness; therefore, the attorney argued, she needed her daughter's help in the US. As Hing (2004) and de la Torre et al. (2010) have noted, criteria for adjusting status after unauthorized entry into the US has become increasingly stringent and require demonstration of extreme or unusual hardship or beyond that which would be expected as a result of separation from a loved one. The family's situation was complicated by Luis' deportation and Angela's "voluntary departure." However, the attorney could demonstrate with the help of medical and mental health experts that both Angela's mother and Gabriel in Mexico were experiencing extreme hardship. Angela and the children were able to return to the US two years after their departure. Gabriel could not graduate with his class because he lacked the credits. He had to obtain a GED before he could apply to college. He continued to be depressed and unmotivated, so he took a job at a gas station, vowing to return to school when his father rejoined the family. Lolita began high school, but "life never was the same"; her friends had moved on to other relationships and she had to rely on her cousins and brother to make sense of what had happened.

With their father still back in Mexico, he and the children remained separated from each other for three more years. Angela struggled with depression and a pervasive shame that they had been treated like criminals; Luis had been chained and handcuffed prior to his deportation. Her parents as well as Luis' lived with the guilt that they had brought their children to the US as teens to give them a better life but, in so doing, had broken laws that ended up criminalizing their children and separating the family. In Mexico, Luis also struggled with depression as he could not find work. He migrated to the border and sought work in Tijuana so that, when finances allowed, the grandparents could bring his US citizen children for a visit. Five years after his arrest and deportation, Luis returned to the US "a broken man"; although the children were happy to have both parents with them, the disruption in family life they had endured left an indelible mark on all of their lives.

Mixed status families can also face the precarious process of the documented spouse attempting to adjust the status of his or her unauthorized partner. This legal process also entails documenting unusual hardship. For many Latinos, the waiver process, that is, the unauthorized immigrant's petition for a pardon and a waiver of inadmissibility, can open childhood wounds if they themselves were children of transnational immigrants who often were away from the family. This is particularly the case when children were left behind and experienced adverse circumstances as did Veronica.

Veronica's Story

The youngest of five children, Veronica was left by her parents in El Salvador when she was four years of age. She and her older sisters and brother were left in the care of their maternal grandmother. Veronica described a painful childhood; her grandmother was a stern, negative woman who mistreated them physically, verbally, and emotionally. An uncle who lived with them brought home male friends who sexually abused her. At age eight, she, an older sister, and her brother left El Salvador hoping to reunify with their parents. She and her sister were caught at the border while trying to enter the US without inspection. They were sent back to El Salvador. Her brother was separated from them and kept by a Mexican family who saw what had occurred. Veronica's mother thought her son had been lost forever. This was a stressful and painful period; Veronica was frightened and confused. She did not quite understand why they had left El Salvador and traveled so far to see parents she did not even remember.

After a successful entry into the US a few months later, Veronica was reunited with her parents. However, she did not remember them and had difficulty adjusting to family life, particularly since her father was physically abusive towards her mother. Her mother, still distraught about her son's disappearance, did not ease Veronica's emotional distress. As a result, Veronica had to become self-reliant; she grew into an adult who tried not to feel her emotions and attempted to block painful memories of her childhood.

Veronica became a single parent at age 20. She had a daughter, Jazmin. Veronica later married, "but the marriage did not work out" largely due to her distrust of men and her fear of intimacy, which is the result of her childhood sexual abuse. She separated in 2005 and divorced in 2006. From her early 20s, she worked as a janitor at a college campus. In 2010, she met her second husband when he came to the campus to work as a painter. Antonio, originally from Leon, Nicaragua, came to the US in 2008. They married in 2011 and had a daughter a year later. Given the precarious work situation he experienced as an unauthorized migrant, Veronica decided to adjust his status. She became a citizen and petitioned for her husband.

The I-601 process[7] and the potential separation from her husband reopened childhood emotional wounds, leading to feelings of loneliness, isolation, and intimacy problems. Veronica complained that since her daughter was born she "pushed her husband away due to flashbacks of childhood victimization and fear that he would have to leave," and she would be alone again. Veronica indicated that she did not know what she would do if her husband was not granted a waiver. Of late, she had become increasingly anxious. She felt that a separation from her husband would constitute another trauma; she did not know if she could cope with it.

Veronica also stated that she could not go to Nicaragua with her husband. She had never been there. Her daughter was doing well in school and her baby had good health care available through her job in the US. She did not want her daughters to experience the poverty and violence she did during her early childhood. Therefore, she and her daughters would remain in the US. However, she would be alone and bereft again. She already had experienced the hardship of being a single parent. Veronica could not bear the thought of being a single mother again. The mere thought of a separation from her husband was profoundly devastating.

As a result of her victimization in childhood and the dysfunction in her family of origin, Veronica had learned to block her emotions and detach from strong negative feelings; moreover, she believed that if she sought mental health services, it would signify that she was weak.[8] However, Veronica agreed to enter therapy since acknowledging her distress and seeking mental health services could be an avenue to document the extreme hardship that a separation from her husband would cause. In therapy, her history and the sequelae of her victimization in childhood could be documented; a psychological evaluation also could explain how those experiences could result in extreme hardship if her husband was not granted a waiver. In this case, the difficulties inherent in being in a mixed status family and initiating the waiver process opened the door for healing to begin. Regardless of the outcome of the immigration case, psychotherapy could be beneficial and act as a pathway for her to learn more effective coping mechanisms that could break the parenting and partnering patterns she had learned in her family of origin.

DEPORTATIONS, EXCLUSIONS, AND DIVIDED FAMILIES

Several of the cases described above illustrate the suffering of adults and children that result from deportations or exclusions based on unlawful entry. When families are divided, a pervasive sadness occurs among adults and children (Miranda et al. 2005). Children who are left when young typically feel that they were abandoned since they may not understand the notion of "legal immigration status" or why their parent(s) had to leave. Older children may experience anger/rage and sadness (Diaz and Lieberman 2010). Typically, these feelings are manifested at home and at school. Academic underachievement is common as childhood depression interferes with learning. These children also may misbehave. Parents or guardians, at times, do not inform school officials that a parent has been deported due to feelings of shame or fear that they, too, may be deported if someone discloses this information. Therefore, children may not receive the help needed to deal with the family disruption.

Technological advances have made it possible for some families to remain connected despite geographic separation. For example, some fathers and mothers who remain in the US use Skype to speak to their children who are in Mexico with the other parent. In this way, they can see the developmental progress of their children, who, in turn, can see the absent parent. Nevertheless, parents who are separated from their children often tell heartbreaking stories of their children begging for them to bring them "home" or join them wherever they are. Some children begin to express their anger at the absent parent and refuse to speak to them. The parent who remains in the US needs to work to support two households, often finding it difficult to travel to visit his or her family due to economic difficulties. Thus, the children see his or her absence as lack of caring or abandonment, as well. In cases of prolonged separation, sometimes the older children want to return and join the parent in the US. However, they miss their younger siblings and parent. Such return migrations to the US by citizen children invariably result in academic difficulties, anger, and depression

Javier's Story

Javier was 15 years old when his 50-year-old mother, Leticia Lopez, was caught in a workplace raid and arrested. Mr. Lopez and his wife also had three older sons: Joaquin, Enrique, and Danny. The eldest, Joaquin, was born in Mexico and was without status, He came as a baby when Mrs. Lopez crossed the border without inspection to join her husband who had been a transnational migrant since his teens. After his wife's arrest, Mr. Lopez scrambled to hire an attorney to obtain his wife's release but lacked enough funds to pay the bond. Mrs. Lopez was transported from a jail in Sacramento, California, to a jail in San Francisco. By the time the family arrived in San Francisco to see her, she had been sent to a detention facility in Arizona. Two days later, she was back in Michoacán, México, a country she had left 30 years before. She went to live in a *rancho* with her aging parents. Javier, the youngest in the family, was devastated. He wanted to be with his mother.

Mr. Lopez worked long hours and worried that without his wife's supervision, some of his boys would get into trouble. His fears were warranted: Danny had been cutting classes even before his mother left, and shortly after Mrs. Lopez's departure, Joaquin was arrested for DUI. He had been despondent since her deportation and had relapsed into alcohol abuse. As the DUI was his second offense, the arresting officers called ICE. Within a week, Joaquin was deported to Mexico, a country in which he had not lived since nine months of age. On the positive side, the couple's second son, Enrique, born in the US, married, and no longer living at home, quickly took the reins of the family and petitioned for his mother.

When school let out for the summer, Javier joined his mother in Mexico and stayed there for six months. However, he could not attend school because the closest one to his *rancho* was too far away by bus. He also was not literate in Spanish and would be placed back in fourth or fifth grade. He returned to the US and reentered high school but soon became clinically depressed. I evaluated him to document the hardship placed on him by his mother's deportation. Javier was brilliant, a critical thinker, and a great writer. However, his depression caused by his mother's absence, his brother Joaquin's deportation, and his brother Danny's increasingly bad behavior was interfering with his academic and psychological functioning. He felt worthless as a child of unauthorized immigrants; he felt powerless to change his family's situation.

Finally, the family obtained an honest and ethical attorney after they learned that the one they had initially hired had been disbarred for failure to properly represent clients. The immigration process, however, took a long time. Javier continued to struggle with depression and suicidal ideation; Danny was arrested for fighting and carrying a concealed weapon—a small knife—and was incarcerated for several weeks; Mr. Lopez became increasingly depressed and his diabetes worsened; and Enrique attempted to balance his obligations to his wife and sons and to his family of origin, but he felt ill equipped to do so.

The Lopez family, as many others in similar circumstances, may well spend years attempting to recover from the crises caused by the deportation of a family member. These experiences create feelings of regret, remorse for having come to the US, failure because they could not establish themselves with greater economic solvency to provide better for their children, and devastation at the family separation. Fear, anger, and depression are common among the children of such immigrants; those with unauthorized status feel they have limited their opportunities and those despite their citizenship do not feel fully "American" because of their loved one's immigration status and myriad experiences of racial and ethnic discrimination.

IMPACT OF MICRO- AND MACROAGGRESSIONS ON MIXED STATUS CHILDREN AND YOUTH

It is well established that discrimination, prejudice, and the myriad micro- and macroaggressions[9] youth may face contribute to a compromised mental health (see Flores 2013; Falicov 2014). The family, first, and then the school, second, provide both protection and risk for Latino children. Under-resourced schools and educational policies that ignore or disrespect the cultural capital that children bring from their home and home culture create great risk. Racist attitudes and biased assumptions about Mexicans and other Latinos affect how teachers treat students, how students treat each other, and how police respond to Latino youth. Parents who work all the time to provide economically for their children may unwittingly neglect their emotional well-being, thus, exacerbating the stress created by a disenfranchising school climate and daily microaggressions. Parents may be unaware of the disparaging treatment their children receive. Others are fully aware that teachers devalue their children and do not consider their parental involvement in their children's life as important or valuable (Manzo 2014). Moreover, differences in value orientation because of the acculturation and biculturality of their children also pose challenges to immigrant families and create tension between parents and children (Falicov 2014).

Less attention has been paid to the impact of parental immigration status on the psychological well-being of Latino children. The APA Presidential Report (2011) reviews in detail the existing studies and documents the academic and social, as well as emotional costs of immigration policies on immigrant children and youth and those who are children of immigrants (both authorized and unauthorized). Falicov (2014), as well, addresses the long-term impact of parental separation on children left behind when mothers or fathers migrate. Younger children may manifest distress in their bodies, eating disorders (over- or under-eating), depression, nightmares, and academic problems. Older children may show rebelliousness along with the other symptoms. Siblings left behind may hold mixed feelings towards those who presumably have a better life with the parents in the host country. Falicov (2014) also notes, "separation of parent and child intensifies the attachment of the child with the new caretaker, and by extension, with the entire maternal or paternal line, but may weaken the attachment with the biological parent" (p. 115). Reunification, although often desired and anticipated for years, is often fraught with anxiety, conflict, and challenges once it occurs. Such was the case of Veronica that was discussed earlier. Falicov (2014) encourages families to prepare for potential long-term separations and once reunited engage in "catching up narratives," wherein parents and children hear each other's stories of their lives prior to reunification. This is a useful family therapy technique to help families reconnect in mutually satisfying ways.

Often, families are brought into the mental health care system after police or social services involvement as discussed earlier in Maritza's case. Although not separated from her daughters due to migration, Maritza became abusive and lost custody of her children. In addition, she was forced to enter individual and family therapy, which proved helpful to begin a healing process for all. Falicov (2014), among other mental health professionals, suggests a reframing of the adjustment problems that occur after reunification by moving away from "family dysfunctions" and toward problems in cultural transition and family reunification stress. By shifting the burden away from parental behavior to changes in family organization post-migration, parental guilt may be reduced, and children's resentment can be heard without being censored.

Migration and the less-than-hospitable social and educational climate young migrant's encounter may exacerbate the psychological distress caused by parental separation and being left behind. Adults who were left behind as children often recount the difficulties feeling connected again to the absent parent. Long-term separation often creates a breach in the parent-child relationship that cannot be fully mended (Flores 2013).

When youth migrate to rejoin families, they often encounter the circumstances that Hardy and Laszloffy (2005) have identified as leading to anger and violence in children—devaluation for being "foreigners " whether documented or not; disruption of community due to leaving behind caregivers who were parent substitutes, friends, and the familiar environment; and devaluation of losses as parents and teachers may not have the time or the awareness of the importance of the losses accompanying migration. Without support to experience, process, and contextualize their pre-migration, migration, and post-migration experiences, youth may be left adrift. In addition, older adolescent males are often expected to work after their migration in order to lessen the burden on their fathers. As a result, many do not attain sufficient education to prosper in adulthood; they do not master the English language or develop bicultural skills to help them obtain well-paying jobs. Some sacrifice their education so that younger siblings remain in school. Many of these men then experience the sorrow and frustration that their brothers or sisters "do not take advantage of these opportunities and instead drop out of school, become parents at a young age, or join gangs[10]."

Older daughters may find themselves providing child care for younger siblings they had not met prior to rejoining their mothers or fathers. Some describe feeling like "Cinderella" before the Ball. Few recognize the parental stress felt by their progenitors who sometimes work two jobs to keep the family afloat financially and, therefore, do not have the time to help their children adjust to their new life. Others meet stepfathers whose existence they did not know and may feel resentful towards, even though they may have been the ones who sponsored them or paid for their travel. In such cases, clear communication and "catching-up narratives" are essential to help integrate the newly arrived into the family.

In sum, it is critical that educators and health care providers understand the context of immigrant families affected by immigration policies; they may be in a position to promote family well-being by supporting the family's efforts to reunify as well as the children's efforts to become members of the school and family community. Furthermore, school curricula that respectfully address Latino diversity and the challenges faced by immigrant families and children can do much to prevent marginalization and feelings of not belonging so often experienced by mixed status and immigrant children.

"NI DE AQUÍ NI DE ALLÁ," ROOTING AND BELONGING IN THE CONTEXT OF "OTHERNESS"

Children of immigrants, whether born in the US or not, often describe feelings of otherness; sometimes these are caused by microaggressions when they are asked their national origin—the assumption being that due to phenotype or accent or skin color they could not be United Statian. Young children may find the question confusing; teens may respond with irony or anger. For most of my adolescence, I was posed that question time and time again. Sometimes it was a crude "what are you?" Other times it was "where were you born or where are you from?" Initially, I would answer it without much commentary. As I grew older and more aware of racism in this country, I would answer more defensively or pose a question of my own: "How much time do you have? Because to answer your question, I have to tell you a story of multiple migrations." Few people really cared to hear the story and would simply walk away.

Gloria Anzaldua (1987) offered that children of Mexicans (and I would add, any Latino) must construct their own identities and become the new *mestiza/os* because we often feel, or are made to feel, that we are neither "from here nor there." In a world of binaries, despite globalization and transnational migrations, hegemonic notions of nativity prevail. In the popular imagination, "American" citizenship is usually accorded to whites whose ancestors came from Europe; everyone else is foreigner whether born on US soil or not. Therefore, identity formation is complicated for youth of color (Hurtado and Gurin 2004), especially those who are mixed race or who do not look "white" (Hills Collins 2009; Root 1996).

For many immigrant Latino parents, the ethnic identification of their children may be a source of confusion, if not concern. In a particularly heated family therapy session, the exchange between Mr. Gonzalez and his son, Juan, a sophomore in college, was as follows:

> **Mr. Gonzalez:** *Que son esas chingaderas de decir que eres Chicano. Eres Mexicano*[11].
>
> **Juan:** Dad, I have never been to Mexico, I don't want to go to Mexico. I don't eat beans and I hate tacos. I was born in the US and have to deal with all the assumptions people have about Mexicans. I am not from there; but I am made to feel that I am not from here either. That is what a Chicano is, Dad, someone who has that consciousness; someone who is aware of the racism we experience because we are children of Mexicans. But you know what, if I went to Mexico they would not want me either. There they call us *pochos*[12].

Mr. Gonzalez turned to the therapist and complained that his son never answered in Spanish, which he viewed as a sign of disrespect. Frustrated, Juan retorted that he went to English-only schools, his parents worked all the time, and he did not have anyone to teach him Spanish. He had to learn English in order to do well in school and to be treated better. That had helped him get into college. What more did his father want?

Such exchanges are common between US-born youth and their immigrant parents. Often, neither fully understands the context and experiences of the other. Falicov's (2014) and the other therapy approaches, as outlined in earlier chapters, facilitate the negotiation of differences within the family in order for all family members to feel respected, heard, and understood.

The intersectionalities of race, ethnicity, gender, sexuality, and nativity need to be understood by all family members in order to adjust to the increasing demands of a more globalized world; at the same time, they need to preserve the cultural traditions and values that have helped them survive as a system, despite the adversities and challenges related to poverty, migration, and disruptions brought about by family separation.

HOMEWORK ASSIGNMENT

- Reflecting on the movie *Mi Familia*, identify the micro- and macroaggressions experienced by the male protagonists. In what way, if at all, do these differ from those experienced by women?
- Reflect on any of the migration stories you have heard in your family as you answer the following questions
  - What are the major challenges that mixed status families encounter in accessing education or health care? (Draw on readings, lectures, and/or films you may have seen.)
  - In your family, what are the major intersectionalities affecting young people?
  - What are additional stressors/challenges queer immigrants may face? (Draw upon additional readings and previous chapters to answer this question.)

ENDNOTES

1. These losses and gains are ambiguous because there are typically no rituals to denote the departure; the losses entail leaving behind intangibles as well as loved ones with the expectation and hope of attaining gains at some future time—the American dream—which may or may not occur. There is, at times, a feeling of shame about leaving in the midst of the excitement and anxieties about the journey. As Sluzki has noted and was described in earlier chapters, what occurs in the journey and how prepared for the migration the immigrant is will mitigate the challenges of arrival and settlement.
2. For a historical review of this program, see *The Bracero History Project*. University of Texas at El Paso, online at: http://braceroarchive.org/. 2011.
3. For a discussion of immigration policies after NAFTA, see Douglas S. Massey, "March of Folly: U.S. Immigration Policy after NAFTA," *The American Prospect*, No. 37.
4. Migration is a phenomenon that has occurred since the beginning of time; the focus in this chapter is on contemporary migrations in the twentieth and twenty-first centuries. Clearly, European migration to the Americas left a legacy of migration for future generations as well as the sequelae of colonization, genocide, and trauma (see Flores 2013).
5. Civic groups may form in the US to raise funds for maintenance of churches, building clinics, or child care centers "back home."
6. For a multi-media essay on Mayan migration, see Brown and Oden, "Living Across Borders: Guatemala Maya Immigrants in the US South," online at: http://www.southernspaces.org/2011/living-across-borders-guatemala-maya-immigrants-us-south#sthash.c2BWVRSI.dpuf.
7. The I-601 waives the "unlawful presence" and "misrepresentation" grounds of inadmissibility for foreign nationals if they can demonstrate that their US citizen or lawful permanent resident spouse or parent would suffer "extreme hardship" if the foreign national is not allowed to remain in (or return to) the United States. A US citizen's fiancé(e) may also be a qualifying relative for

purposes of the waiver. Unlawful presence is defined as any period in which a foreign national is present in the US after expiration of his or her period of authorized stay (e.g., after the expiration date found on his or her I-94 entry/departure card) or after entering the US without being admitted or paroled (e.g., after entering the US illegally without inspection). The "unlawful presence" ground of inadmissibility typically poses a problem for spouses of US citizens who entered the US illegally without inspection (e.g., through the US-Mexican border), online at: http://www.uscis.gov/i-601.

8. See Y. Flores, 2013, *Chicana and Chicano Mental Health: Alma, Mente y Corazon*, Tucson AZ: University of Arizona Press, for a discussion of Chicanos and Latinos explanatory models of mental health.
9. Psychologist Derald Sue used the term microaggressions to refer to the brief and commonplace daily verbal, behavioral, or environmental indignities, whether intentional or unintentional, that communicate hostile, derogatory, or negative racial slights and insults toward people of color or those who are different on the basis of gender, ethnicity, sexuality, or ability. Macroaggressions can also include unequal wages for men and women, substandard schooling in poor communities, and police profiling of men and women of color. For more information, see Derald Sue, 2010, *Microaggressions in Everyday Life: Race, Gender, and Sexual Orientation*, NY: John Wiley and Sons.
10. This is often a concern of my male clients who seek psychotherapy or immigration-related evaluations.
11. "What the hell do you mean by saying you are Chicano. You are Mexican and that is that."
12. Pejorative term used in Mexico to refer to US-born children of Mexicans who do not speak Spanish well and who "act" like United Statians.

CHAPTER 6

(RE)BUILDING HEALTHY FAMILIES

In the preceding chapters, I have described the multiple challenges that migration, acculturation, and discrimination in all its forms can present to Latino families. I have also reviewed several theoretical models that inform clinical work with Latino families in distress, specifically Celia Falicov's MECA model, developed in the 1990s and refined and updated in 2014, Ivan Boszormenyi-Nagy's Contextual Intergenerational Model, Sal Minuchin's Structural Model, and the narrative- and justice-based approaches developed in Australia and New Zealand. Although the latter methods of understanding and treating families were not specifically developed for Latinos, as was MECA, they have applicability because they take into consideration the context of families and the threats to family well-being that emerge from injustice and disparities.

In this chapter, the focus is on working with families who want to heal from injustice that may be historically rooted and intergenerationally transmitted or from present day policies, such as immigration laws, and discriminatory practices that reflect colonial, patriarchal, and hegemonic views. The first section provides an overview of my clinical work with trauma survivors; by utilizing a case example of a family affected by war, intimate partner violence, and histories of genocide, I underscore the importance of mobilizing systems of support and identifying culturally appropriate healing practices. The next section offers narrative-based strategies for re-scripting narratives of pain in clinical work with couples in distress. The third section of the chapter offers strategies to rebalance intergenerational accounts in families affected by substance abuse and violence. Lastly, a discussion of the importance of promoting justice within the family closes the chapter.

HEALING FROM TRAUMA

Amoridolor, a term coined in the 1970s by Chicanos in Texas, reflects the fact that many of us love so deeply we "feel the pain from the suffering of our generations" as well as the Earth, writes Inés Hernández Ávila in the foreword to Elisa Facio and Irene Lara's (2014) *Fleshing the Spirit: spirituality and activism in Chicana, Latina, and Indigenous women's lives*. Indeed, the pain created by historical oppression and injustice may be coded into our DNA and influence how we experience and deal with contemporary trauma.

This *amoridolor* may manifest as impatience, despair, depression, *nervios*. We may cope through prayer, avoidance of the memories, dissociation—separation of mind/body/spirit—and become susceptible to outrage that explodes into violence. We may also feel that we are unlucky and undeserving of being loved in respectful and healthy ways. After she was raped at a college campus by another Chicano, a young woman wept and stated, "I am one more, one more in the long chain of victimized women in my family. It goes back to when the *españoles* came. *Siempre seremos las chingadas* (we will always be the violated ones)." Her despair was augmented by the knowledge that her victimizer was a *carnal*, a "brother." She understood that he, too, was a victim "of the system," which made it all the more difficult to report the crime.

As stated in earlier chapters, historical trauma weighs down on the generations that follow, creating risk factors for family injustice and individual and collective suffering. In collectivist cultures, when one suffers, everyone feels the pain. Thus, individual pain reverberates throughout the family system. While individual family members may respond differently to the trauma, to varying degrees everyone experiences it. Therefore, healing often occurs best in family and in community; this was at the root of the *cultura cura* (culture heals) consciousness of the 1970s and 1980s that informed the movement to provide culturally attuned and responsive services (Flores 2013).

Central to healing from intergenerational trauma is to **know** the history in order to **understand** *el por qué* (why things happened) and then to **change** the legacies. In my work with families, we mobilize storytelling. I invite the adults to tell the story of how they became a couple/family, and then each tells the other and their offspring how their own families of origin came to be. If grandparents or other elders are available, they, too, are invited to share their stories. In this way, the younger generations begin to learn not only their family's history but also their cultural/national/racial/class origins. Then, together, they make a family tree. The genealogy is begun in the office but continued at home. I usually tell families that every family system has a genealogist and invite them to inquire who in their extended family holds that role. This is particularly helpful when the family in treatment knows little of their origins. Someone always knows something and is waiting to be asked. If long-term disconnections have occurred, I invite the family, especially if they have US-educated children, to do some research about the town, city, and country from which their ancestors came. I invite them to read novels and hold family meetings to share what they have learned. In this way, communication increases, elders feel valued because they are included, parents feel their history is validated, and younger ones become more rooted into their culture of origin, which is an antidote to the psychological homeless caused by discrimination and racial oppression in the United States.

By analyzing their genealogy, family members begin to visually observe when the "problems" or injustices began among their ancestors. They also can identify patterns of resilience. If, suddenly, someone begins to manifest problematic drinking, the family is asked to hypothesize what might have happened to cause it. Family members become researchers and chroniclers of their own family history. Key questions are explored: Who has held the role of identified patient in earlier generations? Does the current holder of that role manifest similarities in birth order, gender, sexuality, and color to those who previously held those roles? In families that have migrated, I ask family members to identify migration-related roles. Who is the mourner? Who is the over- or underacculturator? Who in the family is expected to continue the legacies of success and of suffering? As the MECA model suggests, family dysfunction may be related to changes in meaning systems post-migration and losses, mourned and unmourned, as a result of leaving the homeland; intergenerational and value conflicts as a result of migration; and the loss of the cultural niche and difficulties in forming or integrating into a new one. These challenges are primarily manifested among immigrants while depression and anxiety disorders may be more prevalent among the children of immigrants (Flores 2013; Sluzki 1979).

The treatment goal is to make the invisible, visible—a Contextual Intergenerational Family Theory technique. In this way, family grand narratives or organizing principles are made visible to all. Often, there is an "aha" moment when the family members begin to make sense of previously puzzling family patterns or beliefs.

My mother had a saying that echoed throughout my childhood and adolescence: "Once we were rich, once we were white, once we were French, but because men mess up everything they do, we are now poor and colored." As I got older, I wanted to know what she meant by that. Her grandfather Antoine Perigault had migrated from France with his young wife in the late 1800s to build the Panama Canal. His wife quickly succumbed to malaria and died. He then met a young woman in Panama who was of German ancestry, Ana Nücher. They married and had two children, Alfonso and Antonia Perigault Nücher. Antoine and Ana gave their children Spanish versions of French names. Over time, Antoine became a successful business owner of bars and gambling houses. Antonia became educated and married an Afro-Panamanian man, who became a famous writer. Alfonso worked in his father's businesses but had a penchant for drinking the profits and womanizing. He married a *mestiza/mulata* woman, Maria de las Mercedes Medina, whose father was a Spaniard and whose mother was black and indigenous. Alfonso carried his parents' unresolved migration traumas and histories of losses, and he abused alcohol. In an alcoholic state, he was often violent. Some of my mother's childhood memories are of his rages wherein he would destroy the sewing his wife had worked on to sell in order to help the family economy; thus, Alfonso's drinking and gambling made him a poor provider. My mother cowered in fear, full of love and pain—*amoridolor*—for this man.

My maternal grandmother was a strong woman who fought back against her husband's rage; but my mother became a sad, quiet, anxious child. Her parents' marriage was volatile; her parents often separated but quickly reconciled, and when my mother was seven years old, her father died. My grandmother had known nothing of the business and was left destitute. Therefore, she put my mother in convent school, and Mercedes, as she preferred to be called, and her nine-year-old son worked full time to support them. Therefore, my mother grew up alone and mistreated by racist Spanish nuns who disliked poor children. Mother developed a grand narrative that men were not accountable and reliable. Therefore, women must study to be financially independent. She became a teacher and married young. She was unaware that her first husband, who fancied himself a poet, was also a gambler. After she had two sons with this man, she left him and went to live with her brother and his wife.

As I grew older, I called into question my mother's views of men because my father, her second husband, had been the perfect financial provider. It was not until I learned the story of my grandfather Alfonso that I fully understood her views. But her grand narrative invisibly influenced my life decisions: with whom I partnered, how I lived my marriages, and how I left and was left by men I loved. Although I taught my children their family history, the power of the legacy has continued. My daughter married the son of a mixed-raced couple. My son-in-law's father is Afro-Caribbean and German. While my mother minimized her German and African roots, my grandchildren carry a German surname and are proud to be Afro-Latinas. They represent the racial tapestry of the Americas; the eldest looks indigenous Mexican, like her mother and paternal grandfather; The middle child looks more Afro-Latina, like her paternal grandmother; and the youngest, a boy, is the lightest of the three with golden curls. As they grow up in the United States, my grandchildren will undoubtedly face the colorism[1] that affects Latino families, which is a direct legacy of conquest, colonization, and racial mixing.

As a graduate student, I studied my own family history to uncover the secrets and mysteries that had invisibly affected my generation. It became obvious to me why I had chosen psychology as a profession and how I had ended up working in substance abuse services and family violence programs—I have been trying to heal wounded men and thereby understand and exonerate the pain of my maternal grandfather. My life work has been with immigrant families and their children. This is a legacy of the *amoridolor* of my family.

Both as an educator and a practicing psychologist, I view the problems families present in treatment as rooted in historical legacies; consequently, understanding one's history is paramount in order to heal and to change dysfunctional patterns of behavior. Thus, in treating trauma, I primarily utilize the Contextual Intergenerational Family Theory model. As stated in earlier chapters, family problems must be understood through a contextual analysis of the families historical realities, migration and its legacies, the particularities of an individual's experience and the psychological sequelae of the legacies, and the unique experiences of the family members, as well as how the individual gives meaning to his/her experience and historical realities. Likewise, it is also essential to understand the family's co-created scripts and roles (mourner, overacculturator, etc.). I often see family problems as psychological manifestations of historical facts.

These psychological manifestations occur at both the individual and family-system level. As noted in previous chapters, families in distress typically manifest parentification, triangulation, and imbalanced levels of involvement—either cutoffs or over-involvement—as well as cultural freezing and problems in adaptation to life cycle changes, migrations, separations, etc. "Problems" often become visible after a life cycle transition, such as marriage, birth of a child, divorce, or death of a loved one. Moreover, trauma is often rooted in relational injustice—exploitation, family or intimate partner violence, infidelity, and economic control. In turn, relational injustice is rooted in legacies of miscegenation, oppression and pain, legacies of migration, imbalances in debits and merits, over- or under-entitlement and destructive entitlement, and lack of reciprocity.

Thus, the goal of treatment is, first, to understand the historical roots of the problem and how these legacies affect each and every family member; second, to address the individual needs of family members and promote his or her individual healing, particularly of the identified patient; third, to encourage systemic change to improve family relations, create greater balance in debits and merits and promote reciprocity, and to mobilize compassion and forgiveness within the family; and last, to promote *concientización* (consciousness raising) within the family so that through their actions and efforts at change a new legacy is created for future generations. My work with the Luna family helps illustrate this approach.

Elba and Nestor Luna

Elba and Nestor Luna, a couple in their early 30s, sought therapy because Nestor was having "anger management issues." Elba had insisted on therapy as a condition to remain in the marriage. Elba is a US-born third-generation Latina of mixed parentage. Her mother immigrated from Ecuador as a teenager with her mother and four sisters. She became an educator and married a second-generation Chicano and Vietnam War veteran. They had Elba but divorced because her father had "difficulty being married." Elba's father was a mental health professional. Elba's mother remarried "a very nice Peruvian man" who was also an immigrant. Elba also became educated and married an immigrant from El Salvador who was a political refugee and whose immigration status was pending[2].

Since the early days of the marriage, the couple had cultural and linguistic conflicts. Elba felt more comfortable speaking in English and Nestor preferred Spanish. He was very supportive of his wife's educational aspirations and career plans partly because his forced migration had prevented him from pursuing his own studies. However, Elba felt unsupported because in her view, her husband had unrealistic expectations of her, which were cultural- and gender-based. He was neat and liked an organized home. He could not tolerate the chaos that her piles of paper and son's toys created in their home. She did not prioritize having a clean home and felt that working, going to school, and parenting were enough work for one person to do. Although her husband helped with housework, he became frustrated when she did not keep up with his efforts at cleanliness and organization. He felt that she did not respect him; she felt that he did not understand her. They also had conflict because Nestor and his in-laws disagreed on parenting practices once their son was born.

Elba temporarily separated from Nestor when, during an argument, he punched a hole in the wall. She became "terrified of his violence" and moved in with her mother and stepfather. The separation from his son and wife was devastating for Nestor, who sought individual treatment for his "anger issues." They did not want to divorce. As a child of divorce, Elba did not want to end the marriage; she wanted him to change. She felt strongly that his behavior was unacceptable and that she needed to protect her son from his father's rigidity and aggression. After a few months, they reconciled, and Nestor moved in with his wife and his in-laws. However, the conflicts regarding parenting amplified once they all lived together. Nestor felt that his mother-in-law was undermining his authority; he viewed her as overly permissive and that she and his wife were spoiling his son. They expressed concerns that his authoritarian discipline was too harsh for young child.

Elba also complained that Nestor was too rigid. He had to go to bed early because he began work at five a.m.; she liked to stay up. Therefore, he would put their son to bed and go to bed alone while she socialized with her mother and stepfather. He felt rejected. She thought his feelings were ridiculous. Another source of conflict was that Nestor liked to eat quietly, and her family used dinnertime as a coming-together and socializing opportunity. Thus, Elba became anxious every day at dinnertime because Nestor ate quickly, did not talk, and left for their room as soon as he was done eating. They often argued about this. On one occasion, their son was making too much noise and Nestor yelled at him at dinner. Everyone was shocked. Elba was ashamed about her husband's behavior in front of her family. She began to consider divorce, discouraged about his "unwillingness to change."

At face value, the "problems" of this family did not seem serious or related to intergenerational trauma. The treatment could have focused on resolving couple conflicts. While it was important to understand their couple conflicts and their feelings of being unsupported and not understood by the other, the extended family involvement, migration histories, and losses related to divorce needed to be addressed. We began by exploring their family histories and paying attention to the historical realities each partner brought to the marriage. Elba shared how her parents' divorce left her feeling insecure. She described her father as very self-absorbed and not really able to "connect emotionally." As he was a war veteran, I inquired about the presence of trauma symptoms. Elba had not really thought about that as he did not like to speak of the war. She had been born post-Vietnam and had not learned much about that war in school. After the session, she asked her mother about whether her father had had any PTSD symptoms. Her mother confided that during their brief marriage, she lived in fear of his moods and that her worries about feeling unsafe had motivated the divorce. Her mother really did not understand his political views or his focus on Chicanos either. She was Latina and comfortable in her identity; she could not understand her ex-husband's "chip on his shoulder" about his ethnicity.

Nestor did not like to talk about himself, his family, or his migration. He was reluctant to talk about his life in El Salvador; when he did, he disclosed a difficult childhood. His parents were married but lived apart. His father liked living in the country in his farm where he raised animals. His mother liked the comforts of the city. She ran a small business and was rarely home. Nestor ate alone in the kitchen with the maid. This was the root of his discomfort with family meals at his in-laws. He was a sullen child, by his own account, but enjoyed visiting his father in the country. His father was a man of few words, so when they were together they spent their time in quiet companionship. Nestor had learned to be a man by observing his father's isolation, strong work ethic, and quiet presence.

When Nestor was studying at the university, he had friends who were politically active. As a result of this association, he began to be followed by police who suspected most young university students to have leftist leanings. During the civil war, both the military and the guerrilla targeted Nestor. He refused to join either group. Fearing for his life, his parents insisted that he migrate to the US. Nestor had a few relatives in southern California, so he agreed to join them there. Nestor denied experiencing any violence directly but witnessed the detention and disappearance of friends. He was cut off from any feelings related to this. In one session, he noted, *"Yo no puedo pensar en eso, abriría una fuente interminable de dolor"* (I can't think about any of that; it would open an interminable fountain of pain).

I encouraged Elba to consider the similarities in her husband's and her father's experience with war-related violence and invited the couple to explore how these experiences had influenced their individual psychology and their family relations. Elba suddenly realized that she carried a great deal of fear, which manifested as anxiety that was related to her mother's fear of her first husband's potential violence. Her fear of Nestor's potential violence was connected to that historical reality. She realized that she had married a man very similar in psychological make-up to her father but wanted him to act and be more like her more "modern, progressive, calm" stepfather. Nestor had married a woman "totally unlike his mother," who was physically and emotionally absent for most of his childhood and adolescence; he perceived Elba to be over-involved and over-protective of their son. What Nestor had not consciously realized was that due to their conflicts, Elba was treating him in a more cool and detached way as his mother had during his childhood.

Moreover, Elba also had a history of trauma in her genealogy. Her mother's migration to the US had been the result of multiple family tragedies. Elba's grandmother had three sons who had all died suddenly, accidentally, or violently. Elba's grandmother could no longer bear to live in Ecuador and moved with her surviving children, all girls, to the US. Little was known of Elba's grandfather. The legacy of unreliable men had begun long before in South America and was affecting Elba's relationship with her husband. Moreover, Elba's grandmother was a strong matriarch who exemplified for the daughters and granddaughters the strength required of women to make it in the world. The early losses were not talked about; but the family valued interdependence and frequent contact, unlike Nestor's family of origin that was more disengaged. In therapy, they explored how their own family histories of trauma had nuanced family life.

Nestor loved his wife and child, but he seemed uncomfortable with showing his affection as he had not experienced the *cariño* (caring tenderness) that his wife so freely showed their son. The *amoridolo*r he felt for his own childhood was interfering with his desire to be a good husband and father. He was too stern, unable to balance his love with his desire to shape his son into a strong and noble man. By exploring how their respective family legacies intersected and shaped their relationship style, they became more conscious of their family dynamics. Elba struggled to balance her fears with her trust in her husband. Nestor struggled to be emotionally present when overwhelmed with the sounds of family life.

In order to change how they related as a couple and as parents, Elba and Nestor needed to critically examine their history and cultural practices. Elba was more acculturated than Nestor who wanted to recreate life in his country in a setting that required far more of him—emotional presence, high contact with extended family, less authoritarianism. To accomplish this he needed his wife to support his masculinity and his contributions to their family. Elba was often critical of everything he did and had difficulty pointing out her husband's contributions. Her anger at her father was unfairly directed at her husband. Elba needed to understand how his social position as an unauthorized immigrant marginalized him and led to feelings of disempowerment. He needed to feel valued and important at home. Instead, he felt overly criticized and devalued by his wife and her family. His anger was fueled by his marginalization within and outside his home.

Both felt profoundly disloyal to their families of origin when they began to change, and they engaged in self-sabotaging behaviors. Elba knew how to trigger Nestor's anger, and he knew how to erode her trust in him. This dangerous dance needed to stop for their benefit and that of their son. Extensive reconstructive dialogues (Flores 1998) were encouraged so that each partner could be accountable for his and her part in their problems and commit to mindful coupling and parenting. They both wanted their son to grow up feeling loved and secure, to develop the ability to trust that his parents had his best interests at heart, and to behave accordingly. By shifting the focus to the well-being of their child, both parents could feel less guilty about changing. They examined the gifts they had received from their parents as well as the burdens, and they became more conscious of how their parenting could promote emotional balance in their son.

The couple's cultural differences were also addressed. Elba came to acknowledge that she fell in love with Nestor's *latinidad.* She loved the sound of Spanish as the words smoothly rolled off his tongue while, simultaneously, feeling ashamed that her Spanish was too Americanized. She wanted her son to be bilingual. Nestor resisted speaking English because he felt insecure due to his accent and lack of fluency. His legal status in the US and his accent interfered with his ability to feel that he belonged in his new country. Moving into a bilingual household where both languages were spoken fluidly triggered Nestor's feelings of belonging and loss. We spoke about how living in the borderlands is challenging but also provides the opportunity for co-creating multiple flavors of *latinidad.* Their son was Ecuadorian, Salvadoran, Chicano, and United Statian. We discussed what that mean to each of them, what cultural gifts could come from such rich cultural legacies. As an immigrant and a child of an immigrant, as direct survivors, and as witnesses of traumatic experiences, both partners showed great resilience. Given the complex world in which we all live, home could be the site of sustenance and love as well as protection. Elba and Nestor were invited to imagine a home and family life where they did not fight other people's wars; instead, they could live in peace.

It was critical to convey to this couple that change is a life-long process. While "symptoms" or problems may diminish in intensity, being Latina and Latino in the US will present daily challenges. Therefore, it is essential to learn more adaptive ways to deal with stress, manage microaggressions, and be emotionally present. Ultimately, both Elba and Nestor needed to feel that they deserved to have a loving marriage; they did not need to divorce to find peace and balance in their lives. Nestor could be loyal to his parents without sacrificing himself. He could be a husband and father who was both physically and emotionally present. Elba could support her husband and be a strong, independent woman. She need not exonerate her father by pushing her husband out of their marriage. They could both create peace at home.

RE-SCRIPTING NARRATIVES OF PAIN

Couples often present with stories embedded within multiple stories; that is, the complaints they bring to treatment reflect the stories and narratives of others important to their lives (i.e., extended families, in-laws) as well as historical issues of justice/injustice. The goal is to develop a collaborative relationship with the partners by posing questions to help externalize the problem in order to deconstruct and reconstruct it. The therapist is less directive in narrative approaches than in other modalities of couple therapy and needs to be aware of social justice considerations, including cultural/familial embedded stories that oppress (for example, *el que dirán*, a preoccupation of what others will think). In such cases, the couple does not own the story; the story owns them. A treatment goal would be to shift to *"Cómo lo diré o Cómo lo diríamos"* (the couple owns the story)[3]. The therapist also ought to listen to narratives of disempowerment and despair as discussed in earlier chapters. The following vignette may illustrate these issues.

Marcos and Elena

Marcos and Elena were both highly educated second-generation Chicano professionals in their early 30s; both were children of working class Mexican immigrants. After six years of marriage, she had separated from Marcos because of his "sexting" to a female friend. Elena moved out and continued with her master-level studies while working full time. Despite the separation, they saw each other occasionally and were often sexually intimate during those meetings. She had agreed to come to a few sessions as long as he was accountable and "fessed up" to how he had ruined her love for him and their marriage.

Elena was ambivalent about divorce but furious at Marcos' behavior. Moreover, she described him as financially immature; despite his good education, he mismanaged money, and she often had to bail him out. She stated that she could no longer be married to a man who could not be financially responsible and who was morally corrupt, as well. Marcos described his wife as rigid, angry, and unwilling to negotiate. Over the course of three meetings, both admitted to infidelity. Marcos was particularly wounded because Elena had invited her lover and not him to a family dinner in honor of her graduation.

She responded that he had gone away for a weekend with his lover when he proclaimed to be trying to work on their relationship. They were at an impasse, full of *amoridolor*.

Since Elena had only agreed to a few sessions and had decided to file for divorce between our second and third meeting, the focus of treatment was on ending their relationship in a respectful manner by understanding how things went awry. This was challenging as neither saw the usefulness of exploring their families of origin or how they had any influence on their relationship. I asked Elena how her husband had learned to be financially immature and seemingly unable to commit to the marriage. She quickly noted that his family was unable to rise from their poverty and seemed very comfortable in their "Mexican ways."

Her family, on the other hand, while still very Mexican, did not devalue success or acculturation. Marcos retorted how this description of his family was "typical" of his wife's demeaning treatment towards them. He added that his family had been unable to attend the wedding because Elena had insisted on getting married at a fancy Mexican resort, which his low-income-earning family could not afford. Elena offered to pay for their expenses, but out of pride (according to her), they had refused. Thus, their marriage began on shaky ground; Elena did not feel accepted by his family. Her family, however, had initially been warm towards him; but after the sexting incident, her brother and sister-in-law had grown cool towards him. Marcos was grieving that he might not be able to see his niece and nephew, children of Elena's brother, once they divorced. He did not want to lose that connection.

Each held a view of their relationship and of each other that appeared unchangeable. I inquired about Elena's hopes and aspirations when they first met and married. Her tone softened and she recalled fondly how she was impressed by his intelligence. She felt at home with him. However, she had become increasingly depressed by his behavior and had begun individual therapy to help her deal with his financial problems and his unacceptable behavior with other women. She had to "close [her] heart to him" in order to go to work, finish her master's thesis, and graduate.

She described her parents as kind and loving, supportive, and proud of her. Because her family, unlike his, she stated, was functional, she grew up believing that everything was possible—to be Chicana, educated, married, and happy. She had believed that Marcos wanted the same. However, he had a lot of educational debt to pay, which, in her view, he mismanaged. Moreover, he had lost a good job because he was unable to keep track of client accounts. He seemed to have difficulty managing money. I asked Marcos what it meant to him to move out of the working class through education. Feelings of disentitlement emerged. He also had great guilt that he did not have to work as hard as his father, who, ailing from diabetes, still had to work as a laborer. He described his mother as loving but stern, not unlike his wife.

Marcos was influenced by a grand narrative that he should not succeed and become "a better man" than was his father, which he equated with having more education and access to income. His problematic relationship with money ensured that he would remain on the brink of financial disaster and functionally working class despite his professional career.

When I asked him when he stopped being a husband and became a son to his wife, he blinked, held his breath, and responded, "When she killed our baby in order to go back to school." She gasped and accused him of "hitting below the belt." They both wept. Elena had had a first trimester abortion three years prior to beginning her master's program; according to her, she had made such a painful and difficulty decision partly because she did not feel secure in the marriage. Marcos engaged in what she considered to be inappropriate text messaging with female friends. She accused him of being a sex addict. He acknowledged that her rejection and criticism of him caused him great stress that "fantasy sex games" with other women helped release. They continued to blame each other.

I invited them to consider what role—if any—their class position and status as multiple minorities had on their relationship problems. They both spoke of the routine microaggressions they experienced as Chicanos and the feelings of disloyalty they had about "making it" out of the *barrio*. Although they had actualized their families' American dream, they still carried feelings of disentitlement. Marcos struggled with his masculinity and how to balance the internalized views of what it meant to be a *macho* with his ideals of how to be a well-balanced modern man. He engaged in sexting as a way to reduce tension, to be *macho* (in the negative sense), and to avenge the dishonor caused by his wife's abortion. Elena struggled to balance her "soft mothering tendencies" with her Chicana warrior persona, which had served her well in her educational trajectory.

Both seemed unable, however, to form a healthy couple relationship. Elena refused to be a loyal, long-suffering wife/mother as the women in her family had been. She had the economic viability to move on and start a new relationship. They did not feel at home in either their professional world or in their family's working class world. Marcos wondered if he was Mexican enough; Elena was not certain that she could remain sufficiently Mexican with her new European American partner. At the end of therapy, they worked on re-scripting their cultural narratives to create more balance in their life; in so doing, perhaps they might be able to have more satisfying relationships in the future.

Unlike some Hollywood movies, not all relationships end happily-ever-after. Elena, justifiably, could not trust that Marcos would not break her heart again. However, by entering another relationship before the marriage with Marcos had ended, she was repeating a pattern. She had been engaged when she met Marcos, and after a night together, broke the engagement and moved in with Marcos. She appeared unable to end relationships without having another man as a life raft despite her independence. She had internalized a cultural message that a woman without a man is not complete. She also struggled with the good girl/bad girl dichotomy and appeared to associate sexual freedom with being a strong, independent woman without regard to how her infidelity might affect the marriage. Marcos struggled with how to be a man as he had internalized very negative stereotypes of Chicano and Mexican men. I encouraged him to engage in individual therapy to work on these issues.

Elena and Marcos needed to heal their spirit and grieve for their unborn child and the death of their marriage. However, they left therapy, as they left relationships, without closure but with more awareness of the social, cultural, and family narratives that influenced them.

REBALANCING INTERGENERATIONAL ACCOUNTS

As stated in Chapter 5, sexual violence within the family often has intergenerational roots that create multiple forms of dysfunction. Histories of oppression create patterns of dysfunction as a result of unfairness, internalized oppression, and outrage. The psychological sequelae of sexual violence include psychological homelessness, symptoms of psychological distress, and unhealthy scripts for living. Furthermore, relational challenges and problems can be a result of historical unfairness.

Injustice affects the mind, the body, and the spirit. Thus, healing may begin mentally, emotionally, physically, or spiritually. Ultimately, the individual must reintegrate mind, body, spirit, and heart. Healing generally begins in the sphere where symptomatology first manifests. Change can and sometimes must occur in how we think, act/behave, feel, and relate to others and ourselves. Treatment needs to address "the twin issues of helping patients," 1) to regain a sense of safety in their bodies, and 2) to complete the unfinished past" (Van der Kolk, McFarlane, and Weisaeth 1996). The foundation of treatment is the safety of the therapeutic relationship. To heal from sexual trauma often requires multiple modalities of treatment and the involvement of various healers. Natalia's story may elucidate these ideas.

Natalia

Natalia sought treatment at the recommendation of her substance abuse counselor who did not feel she had sufficient training to deal with Natalia's psychological problems. The counselor feared that unless Natalia dealt with her trauma, she would continue to relapse. The counselor also felt that there might be cultural issues at play that she could not address as a European American woman. Natalia was 38 years old when she contacted me. She was a second-generation Nicaraguan woman who identified as lesbian. She also was a nurse who worked hospice. Day in and day out she helped men die from AIDS. The work was fulfilling but depressing, so Natalia began to use the narcotics prescribed to the men after the men died. She was afraid that if caught, she would lose her job, her license, and, possibly, her freedom. Natalia had a couple of "close calls" and decided to deal with her addiction to morphine.

Initially in our work together, I focused on building trust. She stated that she had come to meet with me to appease her counselor but really did not think that a psychologist could help with her addiction. I sensed that Natalia needed safety before she could disclose the roots of her depression and drug use. She was very curious about my origins, and when I disclosed I was Central American, she began to talk about her family.

Her maternal grandmother had been a successful businesswoman in Nicaragua but had migrated to the US with her daughter and husband to join a sister who lived in the San Francisco Bay Area. When I asked what might have invited or pulled her grandmother to the US, Natalia stated she did not know. She became pale and appeared to dissociate. I encouraged her to stay in the present and to breathe. When I asked what had just happened, Natalia could not explain. She said she just "left and went off somewhere." This was happening more often and had occurred prior to her drug use; therefore, she did not think these events were related.

I then asked about her family composition in the US. She stated that she lived alone, but her mother and grandmother lived together. She had a brother who was homeless due to alcohol abuse. When I asked her what she believed led to both of them abusing substances, she dissociated once again. She did not want to speak anymore. Over the next few weeks, her drug use increased; she missed both work and her appointment with her counselor who then went to her home and found Natalia nearly unconscious from an overdose. The counselor and I both recommended in-patient treatment but Natalia refused as disclosure of the addiction to enter treatment would compromise her job. She agreed to go on medical leave for work-related stress and focus on recovery.

Natalia saw her counselor three times a week; she saw me twice a week and went to Narcotics Anonymous daily for a period of three months. During that time period, we continued to explore the possible factors that led to her addiction. She recounted that her drug use had increased over the past year. Her grandfather had died, and she found that she could not cry over his death. She felt guilty because she could not grieve. After his death, she began to have flashbacks and physical sensations that she could not explain. When I pressed her for details of these, she broke down and began to describe how her grandfather had sexually abused her from the time she was small child. She had blocked these memories and wondered whether this man also had sexually abused her brother. When her grandfather died, the abuse memories began to surface as disjointed images and physical sensations.

Natalia began to understand why she did not like to be touched and how she would not allow her lovers to make love to her. She had to be in control of the intimacy, and while she enjoyed giving pleasure, she refused to be touched on her breasts or genitals. This often led to break ups as her partners wanted a more reciprocal relationship; they complained that she was too controlling, even in bed.

I asked about the circumstances surrounding the abuse. She recalled that both her mother and grandmother left for work early in the morning and she and her brother were left in the grandfather's care. She did not know why he did not work. She wept and expressed great anger at her mother for leaving her with such a person.

I encouraged Natalia to invite her mother and grandmother to a session to fill in the memory gaps. Natalia wanted to know why he took care of the children, why he did not work, and why she was not protected. Her grandmother, 70, and her mother, 55, attended a therapy session, curious as to why Natalia was in therapy. Once formal introductions and a bit of *platica*[4] took place, Natalia told the women that she had been depressed for years and had become an addict because her grandfather had molested her. At the disclosure, her mother broke down and told us that he had abused her, too. Natalia became enraged; how could her mother have left her with a perpetrator? What kind of mother was she who handed over her daughter to the man who had abused her as a child? Her mother had no answers, only that she needed to work because Natalia's father had abandoned them. Working as a hotel maid, she did not earn enough to pay for a babysitter.

Both women then turned towards grandmother and asked why they had come to the Unites States. Appearing stoic, grandmother said that her husband had been accused of raping children in their hometown and was about to be put in jail. Rather than suffer that humiliation, she left everything behind and came to the US. He followed and she forgave him, hoping that he would change. Both women were appalled. Grandmother stated, *"No se puede hacer nada, todos los hombres son así de mañosos."* (There is nothing one can do; all men have those bad habits.) Both Natalia and her mother contested grandmother's appraisal. All three women wept. Eventually, Natalia's mother begged her daughter for forgiveness and asked what she could do to support her, how she could help. I suggested that from now on they could work on building an authentic relationship without secrets.

Grandmother spoke of life in Nicaragua during the Somoza regime; the only way to survive was to be tough. She had to be strong not to be raped by soldiers. Gender violence was common and unpunished. Her own father had been military and had often beaten her mother. The three women were connected by a history of social and gender violence that began at the time of the conquest. They had survived and been resilient in the US largely by blocking memories and developing "amnesia," but Natalia and her brother had paid the price. They carried the unresolved trauma, guilt, suffering, and despair of previous generations. It was time to break the pattern.

Natalia tried to get her brother into treatment, but he refused. She continued to work on staying sober, and in therapy, we began a lengthy process of healing mind/body/spirit. She wanted to return to work and wanted to manage her depression without drugs. Thus, we focused on healing the mind first. This entails changing the tapes and scripts learned, inherited, or inserted into our consciousness. In cases of incest, such scripts reflect narratives of disempowerment and feelings of not deserving anything better than suffering. Cognitive Behavior Therapy (CBT), developed by Aaron Beck, is a western practice that facilitates cognitive restructuring. The basic premise is that how one thinks about things influences behavior patterns and emotional responses to thoughts and external events. CBT is considered a best practice in the treatment of depression, PTSD, and many other mental health problems (Rothbaum et al. 2000).

However, Natalia did not like doing homework and considered CBT not Latino enough for her. She tried mindful meditation but would become too agitated as she tried to clear her mind. We talked about more indigenous methods, such as rituals to cleanse from the trauma, *limpias* (cleansings) for soul retrieval—to heal the wounded little girl that inhabited her body—and changing her agreements with self and others as articulated by Don Miguel Ruiz (1997). Natalia found the Toltec philosophy inherent in his work to be more compatible with her own worldview and began to practice following the agreements.

To heal her body from years of addiction and the trauma of abuse, Natalia needed to integrate mind and body. Mind/body integration can be achieved through western psychotherapies, massage therapy, art, dance, or movement therapies. Natalia chose to engage in several forms of treatment. She did EMDR (Eye Movement Desensitization and Reprocessing) with her counselor who had recently obtained certification. EMDR is a psychological therapeutic technique used to desensitize and reprocess psychological trauma. It was developed by Francine Shapiro in 1987 and considered best practice for the treatment of PTSD (Bisson, Roberts, Andrew, Cooper, and Lewis 2013; Shapiro 1987).

Natalia also did family therapy work with me. In our sessions, she explored her cultural and sexual identity and how intergenerational trauma had derailed her for a time. Natalia also saw a body worker who helped her release the somatic manifestations of sexual trauma[5].

After a year of sobriety, Natalia felt ready to heal her heart. Healing the heart entails gaining a deeper understanding of how violence affects emotions and, in turn, interpersonal relationships. Emotional healing can be achieved in many ways, including European and indigenous therapies, such as psychotherapy, art and movement therapy, writing, journaling, and Giving Testimony, that is, breaking the silence about sexual abuse. Natalia began to speak out about her history and healing journey in both professional conferences and NA (Narcotics Anonymous) meetings. One day she noted that she had heard herself laugh; it had been years since she had experienced such joy. She rediscovered that the use of humor is essential for well-being.

To heal the emotions and the spirit sometimes it is helpful to hold perpetrators of injustice accountable by naming the offense and demanding redress while not really expecting to receive it. The redress can be symbolic. In one session, she screamed, yelled, and eventually softly spoke to her grandfather. She demanded that from the spirit world he protect her brother who was suffering still from his abuse. She would forgive him, she said, if he guided her brother into sobriety. She worked through the anger and disappointment towards her mother and grandmother by finding compassion for their own suffering. Some years later, when her grandmother became ill, Natalia nursed her until she passed. Her grandmother was able to die in peace because the secret had been revealed, and her granddaughter had become healthy and functional in her chosen career.

Once she felt more integrated in mind and body and feeling that she was more in control of her emotions, Natalia wanted to focus on healing her spirit[6]. Such healing can begin by becoming accountable and changing dysfunctional patterns. By externalizing the problem, blame, or dysfunction, one can begin to de-construct narratives of suffering, facilitate dis-identifying with the oppressor, and stop engaging in self-destructive patterns. Natalia released guilt over her own victimization and focused on healing herself. As ancillary treatments to the "talking therapies," Natalia used prayer, meditation, guided imagery, and visualization. She found that she could take care of and heal her inner child by taking care of herself and spending time in nature or in quiet meditation. Given her profession and the demands of taking care of others, slowing down and staying in present time was essential. Healing the spirit also may entail finding a spiritual path. Natalia came to view her work as a nurse akin to that of traditional healers; she found balance in loving her patients and being present in their transition to the spirit world. After two years of therapy, Natalia "discharged herself," feeling quite healed and integrated.

A few years later we ran into each other at a conference. I was presenting on the treatment of trauma; she stopped and hugged me and showed me her sobriety pin. She was in a healthy relationship and was taking care of her mother, who had severe arthritis and could not longer work. Natalia smiled and said she was happy. After years of suffering, depression, addiction, and despair, Natalia had regained a sense of safety in her body and had continued to complete her unfinished past.

PROMOTING JUSTICE WITHIN THE FAMILY

The scholar/activists of the Family Centre of New Zealand tell us that the lives and relationships of people are shaped by the knowledge and stories that communities of color negotiate and engage in to give meaning to their experiences. These stories and the knowledge they impart have real consequences. They are not merely reflections or representations of our lives. They actively shape, constitute, and embrace our lives. In the preceding chapters, we have seen how dominant stories of *amoridolor* influence the ways in which Latinos form and live in families. Given the low utilization rates of mental health services by Latinos, which need to be more culturally attuned and accessible, and the significant health disparities they face, it is imperative to promote justice within the family, to strengthen family members within the home, and to inoculate them against microaggressions and institutionalized oppression.

In the last 20 years, Chicano, Latino, and European American scholars have proposed prevention methods to strengthen Latino families (Flores 2013); moreover, since the 1960s, Chicano activists and scholars developed Chicana and Chicano Studies programs that impart the knowledge of history, culture, and politics needed to promote self-esteem among Chicano youth. In later decades, Latino Studies programs also were founded to address the realities and needs of the growing population of other Latino groups in the US. In the last few years, a backlash developed in an effort to ban these programs as separatist and a threat to the United States, even though ample evidence exists to the contrary.[7] Furthermore, in the past 20 years, education, health, and government organizations have recognized the important role of ethnic pride and identification in the well-being of marginalized communities.[8]

Parents and educators can do much to promote justice in families and communities. Parental involvement in school and with their children's education is paramount for the academic development of the next generation of Chicanos and Latinos (see Manzo 2014). Healthy, well-balanced families can guide, support, and root their children by promoting flexibility and bicultural identification, both of which are necessary to thrive in a multicultural context (Falicov 2014). Jerry Tello's (1994) *Cara y Corazón: Face and Heart, a Family Strengthening, Rebalancing and Community Mobilization Process* offers culturally rooted tools to educators and family members. A similar program that Tello developed with his colleagues in 1991 specifically addresses strengthening families affected by substance abuse. Community education endeavors can strengthen families and thereby prevent myriad problems that arise post-migration for immigrant groups.

The Family Centre of New Zealand offers us The Journey Metaphor as a tool to promote change; they posit that:

- *Moving from dominant stories about one's life to preferred stories is like making a journey from one identity to another.*
- *The provision of metaphoric maps of the sort of experiences, feelings, and pitfalls than can happen on this journey by other people who have already made it, can play an important part in enabling people to move forward in their lives.*

This chapter has offered metaphoric treatment maps by telling stories of the lives of therapy clients who sought to rebalance relationships, heal from historical and contemporary wounds, and strengthen their families. In the conclusion of the book, I review the challenges that continue to face Latino families and discuss community-based participatory action research strategies to promote family justice and well-being among rural and urban Latino families.

HOMEWORK ASSIGNMENT

1. Identify and write about your dominant story.
   a. What sociopolitical and historical factors account for the development of that story?
2. Develop a preferred story.
3. In what ways can you promote justice within your family?

ENDNOTES

1. The importance of skin color in Latino and other families of color. In some families, white skin is preferred over brown, black, or darker shades. Myriad terms are used in Spanish to denote colorism. Among Mexicans, *huera* is used to refer to people with light skin and is considered a compliment. *morena* refers to brown skin, and *prieta,* to darker shades of brown. Discrimination on the basis of skin color is prevalent among Latinos.
2. Nestor had applied through NACARA, The Nicaraguan Adjustment and Central American Relief Act or NACARA (Title II of Pub.L. 105–100), a US law passed in 1997 that provides various forms of immigration benefits and relief from deportation to certain immigrants who are eligible to apply for political asylum. Online at: http://www.uscis.gov/humanitarian/refugees-asylum/asylum/immigration-through-nicaraguan-adjustment-and-central-american-relief-act-nacara.
3. Yvette Flores and Hector Rivera-Lopez, 2013, "Couples therapy with Latinos," Workshop Presentation at Strengthening Our Roots Conference, Visalia, California.
4. Exchange of greetings and niceties in which many Latinos engage prior to getting to "the real issues" of the conversation.
5. In some cases, healing the body after sexual trauma cannot occur until after the other forms of healing have occurred.

6. Treatment could have begun with healing the spirit, first, or the heart. Natalia chose where she wanted to begin. It was important that she direct the work to connect to her own agency and power.
7. The Mexican-American studies, some of which were later renamed Chicana and Chicano Studies programs, were created out of a federal desegregation case regarding equal education to all students. In 2010, the Arizona legislature passed the anti-ethnic studies law HB-2811 aimed at Mexican-American studies. The law was written by state officials who argued that "such programs promoted racism against non-Hispanic whites, supported ethnic solidarity, and endorsed the overthrow of the government." Online at: http://www.huffingtonpost.com/2013/08/01/mexican-american-studies-return_n_3690144.html.
8. See, for example, the American Psychological Association guidelines for providers of services to ethnic, linguist, and culturally diverse populations, which include:
    - Giving psychological service providers the sociocultural framework they need to consider diversity of values, interactional styles, and cultural expectations in a systematic fashion. They need knowledge and skills for multicultural assessment and intervention, including abilities to:
        - recognize cultural diversity;
        - understand the role that culture and ethnicity/race play in the sociopsychological and economic development of ethnic and culturally diverse populations;
        - understand that socioeconomic and political factors significantly impact the psychosocial, political, and economic development of ethnic and culturally diverse groups; and
        - help clients to understand/maintain/resolve their own sociocultural identification; and understand the interaction of culture, gender, and sexual orientation on behavior and needs.

    Online at: http://www.apa.org/pi/oema/resources/policy/provider-guidelines.aspx.

CONCLUSIONS

TOWARDS THE FUTURE

To prepare for the future we have to look towards the past. We must know our his/herstory and understand our place in the world as Latinas and Latinos of diverse backgrounds, races, ethnicities, countries of origins, spiritualities, religious practices, abilities, political views, class positions, immigration status, and sexualities. We need to understand how our stories of migration potentiated trauma and mobilized resilience. We must remember that our ancestors built civilizations, explored the cosmos, and had advanced mathematical and medical knowledge thousands of years before the encounter with Europeans. We know now that cultural exchange and economic trade existed between Africa, Asia, and the Americas long before Columbus set sail and accidentally arrived on our shores. We have a rich cultural history that is often erased or silenced in US educational institutions. We must pass this history and this knowledge on to younger generations.

We also know that ancestral knowledge survived despite massive genocide during the conquest and the colonial period (Facio and Lara 2014). As a people, Latinos are survivors. Over the past 50 years, Latinos from Central and South America have migrated in large numbers to the United States, joining the Mexicans, Mexican Americans, and Chicanos who had migrated previously or who had always been here. As stated in the introduction to this book and elsewhere (Flores 2013), Latinos are among the oldest inhabitants of and the newest immigrants to the United States. We have always been here, and we shall remain here.

As I write this book, hundreds of thousands of women, children, and youth have entered the United States, fleeing gang violence in their countries[1]. The *Maras* (*Mara-Salvatrucha*) and M-18, ironically, were formed in the United States by disenfranchised offspring of Salvadoran refugees who experienced the marginalization commonly faced by Latino immigrants and children of immigrants (Wolf 2012). They formed *familia* on the streets because their immigrant parents could not provide the guidance and the tools to deal with the disparagement and violence they faced at school and in the community. As did Chucho in *Mi Familia,* these youth rejected their parents' culture without integrating into the US mainstream or forming their own hybrid culture as did many Chicanas and Chicanos.

The police response to these gangs and the deportation of these youths back to El Salvador and Mexico led to the exportation of gang violence to their respective countries. Many of the deported youth had not lived in the countries of their birth since childhood; they lacked the language and cultural knowledge to integrate back into their new homeland. As a result, they reconstituted their gangs, recruiting local youth who were economically disadvantaged or also deported from the US. The *Maras* and similar gangs have expanded throughout the region, causing increased social violence in Honduras and Guatemala (Arana 2014; Wolf 2012). Some gangs have formed alliances with drug traffickers in the region and in Mexico, resulting in the US Department of the Treasury declaring the *Maras* an international criminal organization[2] that poses a threat to the security of the United States.

The unaccompanied minors who are allowed to remain in the United States will need culturally attuned and trauma-informed services in order to adjust to life in their new country without their families and support systems. What we know for certain is that these children will face great academic, social, and emotional challenges, not unlike those experienced by other Latinos, including the Cuban refugee children of the 1960s[3] and the repatriated Mexican Americans who were US citizens but were caught in government raids during the Depression[4]. Mental health practitioners need to adapt their treatment strategies to respond to these children and youth. Mental health treatment must be grounded in social justice to be effective and respond to the needs of traumatized and marginalized Latinos. Celia Falicov's work and the ideas presented in this book may be of immense help.

LATINO FAMILIES IN THE TWENTY-FIRST CENTURY

As we entered the second decade of the twenty-first century, Latinos were no longer a minority in California and other states (US Department of the Census 2010) largely due to the growth of the Mexican origin group. Most Latinos are now US-born, and while overall the Latino population is young, many Latinos are now over age 60. It is expected that by 2050 the Latino population will be 26%, nearly double of what it was in 2010 (16.3%). Clearly, Latinos, especially Chicanos or Mexican Americans, are no longer a minority in numbers. However, as stated earlier in this book, many Latinos continue to face great educational and health disparities. Despite the barriers to educational and health care access, Latinos continue to enjoy relative good health and longevity. Latinos have an average life expectancy of 81.2 years as compared to non-Hispanic whites, with 78.8 years. This health paradox is partly explained by cultural protective factors, which, unless eroded, maintain the physical and emotional well-being of Latinos (Hayes Bautista 2004).

Falicov (2014, 441–442) lists some of the protective factors that maintain Latino families' emotional and relational health; these include:

- Family unity and protection of one another
- Help for those in need (interdependence or mutuality)
- A strong community orientation (collectivism)

- Preserving connection through the life span
- Valuing harmonious relationships (personalism)
- Teaching children the value of endurance and hard work
- Maintaining strong adult sibling bonds
- Dedication to protect and raise the next generation as productive and socially committed citizens
- Enduring separations from loved ones in order to improve everyone's lot
- A spirit of acceptance, struggle, and, ultimately, resilience against adversity
- A religiously or spiritually sustaining faith
- Deeply felt attachment to and pride in cultural traditions
- Respect for the dignity and wisdom of the older generations
- A celebratory spirit that affirms love, life, and joy in the midst of material deprivation

These are the strengths of Latinos families, which must be supported by social institutions, including schools and health programs. As Hayes Bautista (2004) has noted, most second- and third-generation Latinos identify as "American Latinos"; they embrace a hybrid identity; they recognize their "Americanness" while maintaining adaptive Latino cultural values and practices. Educational and social programs that promote and strengthen Latino values can do much to ensure that Latinos will continue to thrive and maximize their opportunities as they face the challenges inherent in majority status within a racialized context that still stereotypes, devalues, marginalizes, and problematizes them. A well-functioning family that maintains the strengths listed above can facilitate the success of future generations.

The Chicano and other social movements of the 1960s brought about a greater *concientización* and a reconnecting to ancestral knowledge(s) and spiritualities. To heal from trauma and unlearn social and gender violence, Chicano men formed men's circles. By sharing theirs stories, learning ancient ways, and being accountable, these men sought to become *hombres nobles,* men in balance. Guided by the Mayan philosophy of the unity of all things and beings, which is reflected in the greeting "*In Lak'Ech,"* meaning "*tu eres mi otro yo"*(you are my other me), many Chicanas and Chicanos promote interdependence and accountability as well as healing *in* community. At the same time, many Chicanas and Latinas have reclaimed their indigenousness and, along with Indigenous women, have begun to foreground their spirituality and spiritual activism (Facio and Lara 2014). Through literature, the arts, and decolonial scholarship, many Latinas and Chicanas began to seek culturally congruent ways to regain and remain in balance with themselves, each other, their *familias*, and the earth mother[5].

ROLE OF EDUCATION AND MENTAL HEALTH IN FAMILY HEALTH PROMOTION

As stated earlier, educational institutions and mental health professionals can do much to promote family well-being. Since the 1970s, various Chicano and Latino agencies were created to provide psychological services to individuals and communities affected by various forms of trauma (see Flores 2013), and mainstream groups, such as the American Psychological Association, have recognized the importance of culturally competent care. Much more remains to be done. As professionals, each of us is accountable to those upon whose shoulders we stood to get ahead. Those of us who have benefited from educational opportunities and have gained the privilege of an education can demonstrate that we did not stop being Latinas or Latinos when we became successful. A commitment to social justice and spiritual activism is necessary for twenty-first century scholarship.

We must contest dominant notions of assimilation, which attempt to erase the rich cultural dimensions of being Latina/o. In her essay, "Latinos and the façade of whiteness," Dana Torres (2014) notes that:

> *Therein lies the problem in the United States, whereby thriving is equated with assimilation into Whiteness. This plays into a fallacious ideology in which Whiteness signifies all that is right in the world, and thus, reinforces the idea that in order to be successful, we must let go of the things that make us non-White and "inferior." In other words, to be accepted and absorbed into the social construction that is Whiteness, we must accept a new pseudo-reality of racial and cultural ignorance.*

She adds that "we are, as Latina/os, also up against forces that do not want us to know who we are. The nation's history books do not document our achievements, tell us our history, nor our genealogical roots." And this is precisely what we must do to prevent psychological homelessness, outrage, and despair.

Instituted in the past decade at the University of California, Davis, the Center for Transnational Health (CTH), directed by Adela de la Torre, has as its mission "to enhance human capabilities through research-to-practice." A number of applied research projects have enhanced teachers' capabilities to work with children in immigrant communities (Flores and Manzo 2013; Manzo, Cruz, Faitis, and de la Torre 2012), and an ongoing USDA-funded grant utilizes community-based participatory research methods to reduce overweight and obesity among rural Mexican origin children (de la Torre et al. 2013). Understanding that health beliefs and practices are culturally nuanced, this study, *Niños Sanos/Familia Sana,* offers multimodal culturally attuned interventions to over 300 children and their families who participate in the research project in a the Central Valley, California, communities of Firebaugh and San Joaquin.

As co-investigator in this grant, I have had the honor to develop family well-being workshops for study participants who are members of the comparison communities and, therefore, are not receiving the nutritional intervention nor the benefits from some of the enhancements offered to the treatment group. In collaboration with Dr. Rosa Manzo, Dr. Hector Rivera-Lopez, Marisol Reyna, MA, and the project participants, I developed a series of workshops aimed to support immigrant families' strengths and provide tools to negotiate life cycle challenges encountered while raising bilingual bicultural children in the US. Workshop topics included: "the impact of migration on family well-being," "family violence," "male mental health," "parenting adolescents," "parenting bicultural children," "women's mental health" and "self-care." The goal is to train participants in these workshops to become trainers themselves and to deliver the workshops to community members. Dr. Manzo is conducting a similar endeavor with families that participated in her education-focused workshops. The project also utilized the arts to engage the community and to demonstrate our appreciation. Two murals were created, and beautiful artwork was used to advertise the workshops.[6]

The workshops were developed based on topics generated by the project participants. We held focus groups and met with stakeholders and *promotores* from the communities to identify areas of need and topics of interest. Few mental health services are available to these families who live and work in rural, isolated communities. Thus, a community education model is useful in providing family psychology concepts that are culturally appropriate and can be utilized by the families on their own.

Projects such as these hold great promise for underserved communities because they are grounded on social justice ideals[7]. Academics, researchers, and practitioners can form partnerships with community members and stakeholders to potentiate research-to-practice. Such practices reflect indigenous research methodologies that were outlined many years ago by Manuel Ramirez III (1998) and, more recently, by Chela Sandoval (2000) and Bagele Chilisa (2012). This book, designed for an undergraduate course on psychological perspectives for Chicano and Latino families, has a similar goal—to provide students and young professionals with knowledge and tools to better understand their own and the families of others. It is offered in that spirit. *In Lak'ech.* You are my other me.

ENDNOTES

1. See Department of Homeland Security statistics and response to what has been termed a humanitarian crisis. Many argue that deportation of these children and youth back to their countries ensures a certain death because the *Maras* have been known to kill those who escape them. Online at: http://www.cbp.gov/newsroom/stats/southwest-border-unaccompanied-children; and in Sonja Wolf, "*Mara Salvatrucha*: the most dangerous gang in the world," *Latin American Politics and Science,* 54, no. 1, pp. 65–95, 2012, and in Ana Arana, "How the Street Gangs Took Central America," *Foreign Affairs*, Vol. 84, No. 3 (May–June), pp. 98–110, 2005.
2. US Department of the Treasury. Treasury Sanctions Latin American Criminal Organization 10/11/2012. Designation Targets Latin American Gang *Mara Salvatrucha* (MS-13)
3. Cuban children were airlifted out of Cuba and brought to the US through Operation Peter Pan ostensibly to protect them from Communist indoctrination. The children were granted political asylum and sent to live with United Statian families throughout the US; many children never saw their families again or returned to Cuba. For an excellent discussion of this program, see Flora M. González Mandri, "Operation Pedro Pan: A Tale of Trauma and Remembrance," *Latino Studies,* 6, 252–268, Autumn 2008.
4. See Eric L. Ray, "Mexican Repatriation and the Possibility for a Federal Cause of Action: A Comparative Analysis on Repatriations," *The University of Miami Inter-American Law Review,* Vol. 37, No. 1, pp. 175, Fall 2005.

5. See Elisa Facio and Irene Lara's anthology, *Fleshing the Spirit: Spirituality and Activism in Chicana, Latina and Indigenous Women's Lives*, Tucson AZ: University of Arizona Press, 2014.
6. See the CTH website for examples of the art team's work at www.cth.ucdavis.edu.
7. According to the RSA, Action and Research Centre, the term "social justice" implies fairness and mutual obligation in society. We are responsible for one another; therefore, we should ensure that all have equal chances to succeed in life, online at: http://www.thersa.org/action-research-centre/learning,-cognition-and-creativity/education/social-justice/what-social-justice-means. In other words, *In Lak'Ech*. For additional UC Davis projects grounded in social justice, visit the Social Justice Initiative funded by the Mellon foundation to address the trauma created by the infamous pepper spray incident on the campus on November 18, 2011, online at: http://socialjusticeinitiative.ucdavis.edu/2014/09/22/october-17-2014-launch-event-global-indigenous-identities-and-alliances/.

BIBLIOGRAPHY

2011 APA Presidential Task Force on Immigration. *Cross Roads: The Psychology of Immigration in the New Century,* 2011. http://www.apa.org/topics/immigration/report.aspx

Aguirre-Molina, Marilyn and Gabriela Betancourt. "Latino Boys: The Early Years." In Aguirre-Molina, Borrell, and Vega, *Health Issues in Latino Males,* (2010): 67–82.

Anzaldua, Gloria. Borderlands/La Frontera: The New Mestiza. San Francisco: Spinsters/Aunt Lute, 1987.

Almeida, R., T. Messineo, R. Woods, and R. Font. "Violence in the lives of the racially and sexually different: A public and private dilemma". *In Expansions of feminist family theory through diversity.* ed. R. Almeida, Haworth Press: New York. (1994): 99–126.

Arana, Ana. "How the Street Gangs Took Central America." *Foreign Affairs,* Vol. 84, No. 3 May-Jun (2005): 98–110.

Bernal, Guillermo and Yvette Flores-Ortiz. "Latino Families in Therapy: Engagement and Evaluation." *Journal of Marital and Family Therapy.* Vol 8 (3) (1982): 357–365.

Bernal, Guillermo and Yvette Flores-Ortiz. "Latino Families in Therapy: Engagement and Evaluation". *Nueva Epoca,* 1, (1984): 2–12.

Bernal, Guillermo and Yvette Flores-Ortiz. "Latino Families: Sociohistorical Perspectives and Cultural Issues". *Nueva Epoca.* (1984): 4–9.

Bernal, Guillermo and Yvette Flores-Ortiz. "Contextual Family Therapy with Adolescent Drug Abusers". In *Family Therapy Approaches with Adolescent Substance Abusers* edited by C.Todd. New York: Allyn and Bacon. (1990): 70–92.

Bernal, Guillermo, Yvette Flores-Ortiz and C. Rodriguez-Dragin. "Terapia Familiar Intergeneracional Con Chicanos y Familias Mejicanas Inmigrantes a Los Estados Unidos (Contextual Family Therapy with Chicanos and Mexican Immigrants)". *Cuadernos de Psicologia.* Colombia: Universidad de Valle. 8 (1) (1986): 81–99.

Bernal, Guillermo., et al. *Development of a Contextual Family Therapy Therapist Action Index. Journal of Family Psychology,* 3 (3) (1990): 322–331.

Bisson, Jonathan, Neil P. Roberts, Martin Andrew, Rosalind Cooper, and Catrin Lewis "Psychological therapies for chronic post-traumatic stress disorder (PTSD) in adults." *Cochrane Database of Systematic Reviews,* Issue 12, 2013.

Boszormenyi-Nagy, I. *Foundations of contextual therapy: Collected papers of Ivan Boszormenyi-Nagy, MD.* New York: Brunner/Mazel, 1987.

Boszormenyi-Nagy, I., and G. Spark. *Invisible loyalties: Reciprocity in intergenerational family therapy.* Second edition, New York: Brunner/Mazel, 1984.

Boszormenyi-Nagy, I. and J. Framo, J (Eds.) *Intensive family therapy: Theoretical and practical aspects.* Second edition. New York: Brunner/Mazel. 1985.

Boszormenyi-Nagy, I. and B. Krasner. *Between give and take: A clinical guide to contextual therapy.* New York: Brunner/Mazel, 1986.

Bowen, M. "Family Therapy in Clinical Practice." In *Family, Violence and Men of Color: Healing the Wounded Male Spirit.* eds. Carrillo, Ricardo and Jerry Tello, NY and London, Jason Aronson, 2nd ed. New York: Springer, 2008.

Burciaga, Antonio. *Drink Cultura: Chicanismo.* Santa Barbara: Joshua O'Dell edition, 1992.

Carter , Betty and Monica McGoldrick. *The Changing Family Life Cycle: a Framework for Family Therapy.* Boston: Allyn and Bacon, 1988.

Carter, Betty, and Monica McGoldrick. "The Expanded Family Life Cycle." *Individual, Family and Social Perspectives.* 4th edition. Allyn and Bacon, 2010.

Castello, A. L. G. *Processamento das experiências traumáticas parentais intergeracionais através do EMDR [Processing intergenerational trauma with EMDR].* In comunicações de pesquisa. Presentation at the 2nd EMDR Brazilian Congress, Brasilia, Brazil, 2012.

Cervantes, Joseph M, Olga L. Mejia and Amalia Guerrero Mena. "Serial Migration and the Assessment of Extreme and Unusual Hardship with Undocumented Latina/o Families." *Hispanic Journal of Behavioral Sciences* 32, no. 2 (2010): 275–91.

Cervantes, Richard C., and Maria Felix-Ortiz. "Substance Abuse among Chicanos and Other Mexican Groups." In *The Handbook of Chicana/o Psychology and Mental Health,* ed. Roberto Velazquez, Leticia Arellano, and Brian McNeill. Mahwah, NJ: Lawrence Erlbaum, (2004): 267–84.

Chilisa, Bagele. *Indigenous Research Methodologies.* Beverly Hills: Sage Pub., 2013.

Chui, Bess, Lynly Egyes, Peter L. Markowitz & Jaya Vasandani. "Constitution on ICE: A Report on Immigration Home Raid Operations." *Cardozo Immigration Justice Clinic.* NY: NY, 2009.

Cuellar, I., R.I. Siles and E. Bracamontes. "Acculturation: a Psychological Construct of Continuing Relevance for Chicano Psychology." In *The Handbook of Chicana/o Psychology and Mental Health,* ed. Roberto Velazquez, Leticia Arellano, and Brian McNeill. Mahwah,NJ: Lawrence Erlbaum, (2004):23–42.

"Culture Shock" (Southern Poverty Law Center 2014) http://www.splcenter.org/getinformed/publications/Culture-Shock

Cunradi, Carol B., Raul Caetano and John Schafer. "Alcohol-Related Problems, Drug Use, and Male Intimate Partner Violence Severity Among US Couples." Alcoholism: Clinical and Experimental Research. Vol. 26, No. 4, April (2002a): 493–500.

Cunradi, Carol B., Raul Caetano, and John Schafer. "Socioeconomic Predictors of Intimate Partner Violence Among White, Black, and Hispanic Couples in the United States." *Journal of Family Violence,* Vol. 17, No. 4, December, 2002b .

de La Rosa, Mario, Elizabeth Y. Lambert, and Bernard Gropper. "Introduction: Exploring the-Substance Abuse-Violence Connection" In *From Drugs and Violence Causes,Correlates, and Consequences,* eds. Mario de la Rosa, Elizabeth Lambert and Bernard Gropper. (1990)1–7.

de la Torre, Adela, Rosa Gomez-Camacho, and Alexis Alvarez. "Making the Case for Health Hardship: Examining the Mexican Health System in Cancellation of Removal Proceedings." *Georgetown Immigration Law Journal* 25, no. 1 (2010): 93–116.

de la Torre, Adela, B. Sadeghi, R.D. Green, L.L Kaiser, Y. G. Flores, C.F. Jackson, S.E. Schaefer, U.S. Shaikh, and L.S. Whent. "Niños Sanos, Familia Sana: Mexican Immigrant Study Protocol for a Multifaceted CBPR Intervention to Combat Childhood Obesity in Two Rural California Towns." *BMC Public Health,* 13, 2013.

Diaz, Manuela and Alicia Lieberman. "Use of Play in Child-Parent Psychotherapy with Preeschoolers Traumatized by Domestic Violence." In *Play Therapy Children for Preschool,* ed. Charles E. Schaefer, 131–56. Washington, DC: American Psychological Association, 2010.

Duran, Eduardo, and Bonnie Duran. *Native American Postcolonial Psychology.* Albany: State University of New York Press, 1995.

Facio, Elisa and Irene Lara. *Fleshing the Spirit: Spirituality and Activism in Chicana, Latina, and Indigenous Women's Lives.* Tucson: University of Arizona Press, 2014.

Falicov, Celia J. *Latino Families in Therapy.* New York: Guilford Press, 2000.

———. *Latino Families in Therapy,* Second Edition. New York: Guilford Press, 2014.

Fuentes, Carlos. *The Burried Mirror: Reflections on Spain and the New World.* Boston: Houghton Mifflin Company, 1992.

Flores, Yvette. *Chicana and Chicano Mental Health: Alma, Mente y Corazon.* Tucson: University of Arizona Press, 2013.

———. "Embodying Dementia: Remembrances of Memory Loss." In Speaking from the Body: Latinas on Health and Culture, ed. Angie Chabram-Dernersesian and Adela de la Torre, 31–43. Tucson: University of Arizona Press, 2008.

———. "La Salud: Latina Girls negotiating identity and making health decisions." In *Latina Girls.* eds. J. Denner and B. Guzman. N.Y.:NY University Press, (2006):199–211.

———. "Parenting." In Encyclopedia Latina: History, Culture, and Society in the United States, ed. Ilan Stavans, 316–22. Danbury, CT: Scholastic Library, 2005a.

Flores, Yvette and Enriqueta Valdez Curiel. "Conflict Resolution and Intimate Partner Violence among Mexicans on Both Sides of the Border." *In Mexicans in California: Transformations and Challenges,* ed. Patricia Zavella and Ramon Gutierrez, 183–216. Urbana: University of Illinois Press, 2009.

Flores, Yvette and R.D. Manzo. "Preparing Teachers to Instruct Latino Students in U.S. Schools." *Teacher Education and Practice,* v.25, 4, Fall (2013): 572–575.

Flores-Ortiz, Yvette. "Desde el Divan: Testimonios from the Couch." *Latina Feminist Group. Telling to Live: Latina Feminist Testimonios.* Durham: Duke University Press, (2001): 294–297.

———. "Fostering Accountability: A Reconstructive Dialogue with a Couple with a History of Violence." In *101 More Interventions in Family Therapy* eds. Thorena Nelson and Terry Trepper. N.Y.:Haworth Press (1998) 389–396.

———. "From Margin to Center: Family Therapy with Latinas" in *Family Therapy with Hispanics* ed. by M. Flores & G. Carey. Boston: Allyn & Bacon (1999b): 59–76.

———. "Injustice in the Family." In *Family Therapy with Hispanics* edited by M. Flores & G. Carey. Boston: Allyn & Bacon (1999c): 251–263.

———. "La Mujer y la Violencia: A Culturally Based Model for the Understanding and Treatment of Domestic Violence in Chicana/Latina Communities." In *Chicana Critical Issues,* ed. Norma Alarcón, 169–82. Berkeley: Third Woman Press, 1993b.

———. "Levels of Acculturation, Marital Satisfaction, and Depression among Chicana Workers: A Psychological Perspective." *Aztlan* 20, nos. 1 and 2 (1993a):151–75.

———. "Migracion, Identidad y Violencia/Migration, Identity and Violence". In *Breaking Barriers: Psychology in the Public Interest* ed. M. Mock, L. Hill, and D.Tucker. Sacramento, CA: California Psychological Association (1999a) 46–59.

———. "My Father's Hands." *In Latina Feminist Group, Telling to Live: Latina Feminist Testimonios.* Durham: Duke University Press (2001):33–38.

———. "Psychotherapy with Latinos: A Contextual Approach". *The California Psychologist.* 24 (4) (1991): 16–18.

———. "RE/membering the Body: Latina Testimonies of Social and Family Violence." In *Violence and the Body: Race, Gender and the State,* ed. Arturo J. Aldama. Bloomington: Indiana University Press, 2003.

———. "The Broken Convenant: Incest in Latino Families." *Voces: A Journal of Chicana/Latina Studies* 1, no. 1 (1997a): 48–70.

———. "The Role of Cultural and Gender Values in Alcohol Use Patterns among Chicana/ Latina High School and University Students: Implications for AIDS Prevention." *International Journal of Addictions,* 29 (9) (1994):1149–1171.

———. "Voices from the Couch: The Co-Construction of a Chicana Psychology." In Living Chicana Theory, ed. Carla Trujillo, 102–22. Berkeley: Third Woman Press, 1997b.

Flores-Ortiz, Y. and Guillermo Bernal. "Contextual Family Therapy of Addiction with Latinos." In *Minorities and Family Therapy,* ed. by G. Saba et. al. New York: Hawthorne Press, Inc. (1990):123–142.

Flores-Ortiz, Yvette, Marcelo Esteban and Ricardo Carrillo. "La violencia en la familia: Un modelo contextual de terapia intergeneracional." *Revista Interamericana de Psicologia* 28, no. 2 (1994): 235–50.

Flores-Ortiz, Yvette, Enriqueta Valdez Curiel, and Patricia Andrade. "Intimate Partner Violence and Couple Interaction among Women from Mexico City and Jalisco." *Journal of Border Health* 7, no 1 (2002):33–42.

Flores, Yvette and Enriqueta Valdez Curiel. Conflict Resolution and Intimate Partner Violence among Mexicans on both sides of the border. In *Mexicans in California: Transformations and Challenges,* eds. Patricia Zavella, D. Segura and J.V. Palermo. University of Illinois Press, 2009.

Flores, Yvette, Hector Rivera-Lopez and Lizceth Brazil-Cruz. *"Mental health and family well being among Mexican immigrant men in rural California."* Report of a PIMSA [Programa de Investigación Migración y Salud] funded grant. Berkeley: University of California Office of the President , 2014.

Guerin, P. *Family Therapy, Theory and Practice.* NY, Gardner Press, 1976.

Guerin, P., T. Fogarty et al. *Working with Relationship Triangles.* NY, London, Guilford. 1996.

Hardy, Kenneth V. and Tracey A. Laszloffy. *Teens who Hurt: Clinical Interventions to Break the Cycle of Adolescent Violence.* New York: Guilford Press, 2005.

Hayes Bautista, David. *La Nueva California: Latinos in the Golden State*. Berkeley: UC Press. 2004.

Herman, Judith Lewis. *Trauma and Recovery*. New York: Basic Books, 1992.

Hernández-Avila, Ines. "Foreword: A Meditation." In *Fleshing the Spirit: Spirituality and Activism in Chicana, Latina, and Indigenous Women's Lives*, ed. by Elisa Facio and Irene Lara pp. xiii–xx. Tucson: University of Arizona Press, 2014.

Hills Collins, Patricia. *Another kind of public education: Race, the media, schools and democratic possibilities.* Boston: Beacon Press, 2009.

Hing, Bill Ong. *Defining America through Immigration Policy.* Philadelphia: Temple University Press, 2004.

Hirsch, Jennifer B. *A Courtship after Marraige: Sexuality and Love in Mexican Transnational Families.* Berkeley: University of California Press, 2003.

Hurtado, Alicia and Patricia Gurin. *Chicana/o Identity in a Changing U.S. Society:¿Quien Soy? ¿Quienes Somos?* Tucson: University of Arizona Press, 2004.

Johnson, Gilbert M and Timothy J. Henderson, eds. *The Mexico Reader: History, Culture, Politics.* Duke University Press. 2003.

Johnson, Michael P. *A Typology of Domestic Violence: Intimate Terrorism, Violent Resistance, and Situational Couple Violence.* Lebanon, NH: Northeastern University Press and University Press of New England, 2008.

Keefe, Susan E. and Amado M. Padilla. *Chicano Ethnicity.* ALBQ: University of New Mexico, 1987.

LaFromboise, Theresa, H. Coleman, and J. Gerton."Psychological aspects of bicultural competence: Evidence and theory." *Psychological Bulletin, 114*, (1993): 395–412.

Manzo, Rosa. *Pláticas de Resistencia: An Examination of the forms of Parent Involvement and Negotiation of School-Parent Tensions in a Farm working Community in California's Central Valley*. Doctoral Dissertation. U.C. Davis, 2014.

Manzo, Rosa, Lisceth Cruz, Christian Faltis and Adela De La Torre. "Teachers of English Learners In Immigrant Communities Special Theme Issue On Educational Opportunity For Immigrant Children: From Preschool To Higher Education." *Mexican-American Educators Journal*, 2012.

My Family, Mi Familia. Directed by Gregory Nava. 1995. New Line Home Video, 2004. DVD.

Miranda, Jeanne, Juned Siddique, Claudia Der-Martirosian, and Thomas R. Belin. "Depression among Latina Immigrant Mothers Separated from their Children." *Psychiatric Services* 56, no. 6 (2005):712–20.

McGoldrick, Monica. *The Genogram Journey: Reconnecting with your Family.* NY: Norton, 2011.

McGoldrick, Monica and Randy Gerson. *Genograms and Family Assessment*, Norton, 1985.

McGoldrick, Monica, Randy Gerson and Sueli Petri. *Genograms: Assessment and Intervention.* Third Edition. Norton Professional Books, 2008.

McGoldrick, Monica and Kenneth V. Hardy. *Re-visioning Family Therapy: Race, Culture and Gender in Clinical Practice*. Guilford Press, 2008.

McGoldrick, Monica, Betty Carter and Nydia Garcia-Preto. *Top of Form The Expanded Family Life Cycle: Individual, Family, and Social Perspectives*. Allyn and Bacon. 2010.

Minuchin, Salvador. *Families and Family Therapy*. Cambridge, MA: Harvard University Press, 1974.

———. *Families and Family Therapy*. Cambridge, MA: Harvard University Press, 1976.

Montalvo, Braulio and Manuel Gutierrez. "The Mask of Culture." A revised version of the chapter that first appeared in *Cultural Perspectives in Family Therapy,* edited by Celia J. Falicov. Aspen Systems Corporation, Rockville, MD, 2001.

National Community Attitudes Towards Violence Against Women Survey, 2009 (NCAS). "The National Violence Against Women Survey". http://www.abs.gov.au/ausstats/abs@.nsf/Lookup/4533.0Chapter24020112009

Nichols & Schwartz. *Family Therapy: Concepts and Methods.* 4th ed. Allyn & Bacon, 1998.

Padilla, Amado. *Acculturaiton: Theory. Research and Some New Findings.* Westview Press for the American Association for the Advancement of Science, 1980.

Passel, J.S. and P. Taylor. *Unauthorized Immigrants and their US born children.* DC: Pew Hispanic Center, 2010. http://pewhispanic.org/files/reports/125.pdf

Paz, Octavio. *El Laberinto de la Soledad.* Penguin, 1997.

———. "The sons of la Malinche." In *The Mexico Reader: History, Culture, Politics* ed. by Gilbert M Johnson and Timothy J. Henderson, Duke University Press. (2003): 20–27.

Peñaloza, Fernando. "Mexican Family Roles." *Journal of Marriage and the Family,*1986.

Portes, Alejandro, and Jozsef Borocz. "Contemporary Immigration: Theoretical Perspectives on its Determinants and Mode of Incorporation." International Migration Review 23: (1989): 606–30.

Quintana, Stephen M., and Nicholas C. Scull. "Latino Ethnic Identity." In *Handbook of U.S. Latino Psychology: Developmental and Community-Based Perspectives* ed. by Villaruel et al., (2009):81–98.

Ramirez III, Manuel. *Multicultural/Multiracial Psychology: Mestizo Perspectives in Personality and Mental Health.* NY: Jason Aaronson, 1998.

Rasheed, Janice, Mikal Rashid and James A. Marley. *Readings in Family Therapy: From Theory to Practice.* Beverly Hills: Sage Publications, 2011.

Restrepo, Dan and Ann Garcia. "The Surge of Unaccompanied Children from Central America Root Causes and Policy Solutions." *Center for American Progress* (2014). http://www.americanprogress.org/issues/immigration/report/2014/07/24/94396/the-surge-of-unaccompanied-children-from-central-america-root-causes-and-policy-solutions/

Rivera Heredia, Maria Elena, Nydia Obregon Velasco, Ericka Ivonne Cervantes Pacheco and Diana Tamara Martinez Ruiz. *Familia y Migracion: Bienestar Fisico y mental.* Mexico: Editorial Trillas, 2014.

Rosales, F. Arturo. "Review of The Treaty of Guadalupe Hidalgo: A Legacy of Conflict." *Great Plains Quarterly*. Paper 578, 1991.

Rothbaum, B.O, EA Meadws, P Resick, DW Foy. "Cognitive Behavioral Therapy ." in *Effective treatments for PTSD: Practice Guidelines from the International Society for Traumatic Stress Studies* eds. EB Foa, TM Keane and MJ Fiedman, NY: Guildford Press (2000):320–325.

Root, Maria P.P. *The Multiracial Experience: Racial Borders as the New Frontier.* Beverly Hills: Sage Pubs., 1996.

Ruiz, Don Miguel. *The Four Agreements: A Practical Guide to Personal Freedom.* Amber-Allen Publishing, 1997.

Rumbaut, Ruben G. "The Crucible Within: Ethnic Identity, Self-Esteem and Segmented Assimilation Among Children of Immigrants." *International Immigration Review. 28. No. 4* (1994): 748–94.

Sandoval, Chela. *Methodologies of the Oppresed.* University of Minnesota Press, 2000.

Savenije, Wim. "Las pandillas trasnacionales o "maras": Violencia urbana en Centroamérica." Foro Internacional, Vol. 47, No. 3, 189, Jul.–Sep., (2007): 637–659.

Shapiro, Francine. *Eye Movement Desensitization and Reprocessing (EMDR): Basic Principles, Protocols and Procedures.* NY:Guilford Press, 1987.

Sinnar, Shirin. "Patriotic or Unconstitutional? The Mandatory Detention of Aliens Under the USA Patriot Act", 55 *Stanford Law Review* 1419, 2003.

Skop, Mariel. "Race and Place in the Adaptation of the Mariel Exiles." *International Migration Review*, Volume 35, no. 2 (Summer 2001): 449–471.

Sluzki, Carlos E. "Migration And Family Conflict." *Family Process*, 18, 4, (1979): 379–390.

Smith, Lorraine and John Winslade. "Consultations with young men migrating from alcohol's regime" in *New perspectives on "addiction"* special edition by Dulwich Centre Newsletter, (1997):16–34.

Souza, Caridad. "Esta risa no es de loca." In the *Latina Feminist Group, Telling to Live: Latina Feminist Testimonios*, 114–22. Durham, NC: Duke University Press, 2001.

Straus, Murray A. and Richard J. Gelles. *Physical Violence in American Families: Risk Factors and Adaptations to Violence in 1845 Families.* New Jersey: Transaction Books, 1989.

Suarez-Orozco, Carola, Dina Birman, J. Manuel Casas, Nadine Nakamura, Pratyusha Tummala-Narra, and Michael Zárate, "Cross Roads: The Psychology of Immigration in the New Century." *The 2011 APA Presidential Task Force on Immigration.* http://www.apa.org/topics/immigration/report.aspx

Tello, Jerry. *Cara y Corazón, Face and Heart: A Family Strengthening, Rebalancing, and Community Mobilization Process.* San Antonio: National Latino Children's Institute, 1994.

Torres, Dana. "Latinos and the Facade of Whiteness." *La Respuesta: a magazine to (Re) Imagine the Boricua Diaspora.* June 11, 2014.

US Census Briefs: "The Hispanic Population" (2010). http://www.census.gov/2010census/

US Department of Health and Human Services: Administration for Children and Families. Children's Bureau. Child maltreatment 2012. http://www.acf.hhs.gov/programs/cb/research-data-technology/statistics-research/child-maltreatment.

US Department of Health and Human Services, SAMHSA, Substance Abuse and Mental Health Services Administration. Newsroom, "National Survey Report."2009. http://www.samhsa.gov/newsroom/advisories/1009152021.aspx

Ramirez, M. "Identification with Mexican family values and authoritarianism in Mexican-Americans". *Journal of Social Psychology*, 73 (1967): 3–11.

———. "Identification with Mexican American values and psychological adjustment in Mexican American Adolescents". *International Journal of Social Psychiatry.* 15(2) (1969): 151–156.

State of Hispanic Girls. Washington DC: National Coalition of Hispanic Health and Human Service Organizations. 1999.

Tello, Jerry. "El Hombre Noble Buscando Balance: The Noble Man Searching for Balance." In Family Violence and Men of Color: Healing the Wounded Male Spirit, 2nd ed., ed. Ricardo Carrillo and Jerry Tello, 37–60. New York: Springer, 2008.

van der Kolk, Bessel A. "Developmental Trauma Disorder." *Psychiatric Annals* 35, no. 5 (2005): 401–9

———. "The Body Keeps the Score: Memory and the Evolving Psychobiology of Post Traumatic Stress." *Harvard Review of Psychiatry* 1, no. 5 (1994): 235–65.

———. "The Psychobiology of Post Traumatic Stress Disorder. Journal of Clinical Psychiatry 58, no. 9 (1997): 16–24.

van der Kolk, Bessel A., Alexander C. McFarlane, and Lars Weisæth. *Traumatic Stress: The Effects of Overwhelming Experience on Mind, Body, and Society*. New York: Guilford Press, 1996.

Waldegrave, C. "Cultural, Gender and Socio-economic Contexts in Therapeutic and Social Policy Work" *Family Process*, 48(1). New York (2009).

Waldegrave C. et al. *Just Therapy—a Journey: A Collection of Papers from the Just Therapy Team*. New Zealand Dulwich Centre Publications, Adelaide, 2003.

Williams, David R., and Chiquita Collins. "U.S. Socioeconomic and Racial Differences in Health: Patterns and Explanations." *Annual Review of Sociology* 21 (1995): 349–86

Williams, David, and Selina A. Mohammed. "Discrimination and Racial Disparities in Health: Evidence and Needed Research." *Journal of Behavioral Medicine* 32, no 1 (2009): 20–47.

Wolf, Sonja. "Mara Salvatrucha: The Most Dangerous Street Gang in the Americas? "*Latin American Politcs and Society*, 54:1, (2012): 65–99.

Yoshikawa, H. *Immigrants Raising Citizens: Undocumented Parents and their Children*. NY.: NY: Rusell Sage Foundation, 2011.

Zavella. Patricia. "Tenemos que Seguir Luchando." In *Latina Feminist Group, Telling to Live: Latina Feminist Testimonios*. Durham: Duke University Press (2001): 348–357.

Lightning Source UK Ltd.
Milton Keynes UK
UKHW050941040921
389864UK00008B/1777

9 781631 891083